RAND

National Defense Researcl

Examining the Cost of Military Child Care

GAIL L. ZELLMAN   SUSAN M. GATES

Prepared for the
Office of the Secretary of Defense

The research described in this report was sponsored by the Office of the Secretary of Defense (OSD). The research was conducted in RAND's National Defense Research Institute, a federally funded research and development center supported by the OSD, the Joint Staff, the unified commands, and the defense agencies under Contract DASW01-01-C-0004.

ISBN: 0-8330-3123-6

Published 2002 by RAND
1700 Main Street, P.O. Box 2138, Santa Monica, CA 90407-2138
1200 South Hayes Street, Arlington, VA 22202-5050
201 North Craig Street, Suite 102, Pittsburgh, PA 15213-1516
RAND URL: http://www.rand.org/
To order RAND documents or to obtain additional information,
contact Distribution Services: Telephone: (310) 451-7002;
Fax: (310) 451-6915; Email: order@rand.org

The military child-care system, the largest system of employer-sponsored child care in the country, has received high marks for providing quality, accessible care for children of military employees. At the same time, the Department of Defense (DoD) is under pressure to control costs and has considered a number of different approaches to delivering care. But efforts to control costs have been hampered by a lack of information on how much it actually costs to deliver care in various settings to children of different ages.

This report presents estimates of the costs associated with providing care to children in DoD-operated Child Development Centers (CDCs), Family Child Care (FCC) homes, and centers operated by outside providers under contract to the DoD. By commissioning this study, the DoD has enabled the first comprehensive analysis of child-care costs across the Military Services. An earlier report on military child-care costs by the U.S. Government Accounting Office focused exclusively on the Air Force, and earlier Service reports on child care provided some cost information, but those reports were limited in their scope. Here, the authors examine cost estimates across Services and across the various age groups served in CDCs and in FCC. To place the study within a broader context, the authors also examine employer-sponsored care provided by civilian employers.

The findings and the recommendations in this report should help military policymakers, military Child Development Program (CDP) managers, and installation-level commands better understand the issue of cost in delivering child care, and help them to determine the best use of resources for the DoD child-care system. This report should also be helpful to civilian child-care policymakers and practitioners, who are increasingly looking at the military system as a model for delivering high-quality care to large numbers of children.

This report is the fourth in a series of RAND reports on military child care. The first, *Improving the Delivery of Military Child Care: An Analysis of Current Operations and New Approaches* (R-4145, 1992), examined military child-care operations prior to the implementation of the Military Child Care Act (MCCA) of 1989. The second, *Examining the Effects of Accreditation on Military Child Development Center Operations and Outcomes* (MR-524, 1994), analyzed a key aspect of the MCCA: accreditation of centers. The third, *Examining the Implementation and Outcomes of the Military Child Care Act of 1989* (MR-665, 1998), analyzed the many changes that the MCCA brought about.

This research was sponsored by the Military Community and Family Policy, Office of Children and Youth, and was conducted for the Under Secretary of Defense for Personnel and Readiness within the Forces and Resources Policy Center of RAND's National Defense Research Institute, a federally funded research and development center sponsored by the Office of the Secretary of Defense, the Joint Staff, the unified commands, and the defense agencies.

CONTENTS

Preface iii

Tables vii

Summary ix

Acknowledgments xvii

Acronyms xix

Chapter One
INTRODUCTION 1
The Link Between Cost and Quality 3
The Role of Quality Standards in Care Delivery 5
Reducing Costs Without Reducing Quality 8

Chapter Two
AN OVERVIEW OF THE MILITARY CHILD-CARE
SYSTEM 11

Chapter Three
STUDY METHODS 21
Installation Cost Survey 24
Sample Selection 24
Survey Sample 26
Survey Form 29
Cost Analyses 29
DoD-Run CDC Cost Estimates 30
FCC Costs 32
Contractor CDC Cost Estimates 33
Civilian Center Visits 34

Chapter Four
    COSTS OF CDC, FCC, AND CONTRACTOR-PROVIDED
    CARE 37
    Costs for CDC Care 37
    Costs for FCC 45
    APF and NAF Expenditures 51
    Cost of Contractor-Provided Care 53

Chapter Five
    AN EXAMINATION OF CIVILIAN-EMPLOYER
    CHILD-CARE CENTERS 61
    Employer Characteristics 62
    Center Characteristics 64
       Management of the Center 68
       Costs and Cost Sharing 72
    Center Programs and Features 79
       General Quality 80
       Employer Motivations, Rewards, and Costs 80
       Program Accommodations to Meet Employer
         Needs 84
    Conclusions 85

Chapter Six
    CONCLUSIONS AND RECOMMENDATIONS 89
       Child Development Center Care 91
       Family Child Care 93
       Contractor-Operated Care 94
       Civilian Employer Care 95
       Implications and Issues 95

Appendix

A. CHILD-CARE COST SURVEY 99

B. REGRESSION ANALYSIS OF COST PER CHILD BY AGE
    GROUP 115

Bibliography 123

TABLES

2.1 Summary of FY 1998 to 1999 DoD Child-Care Fee Report 15

3.1 Categorization of Installations in the Sampling Frame for the Rich and Remote Variables, by Service 28

3.2 Categorization of Installations in the Sample for the Rich and Remote Variables, by Service 28

3.3 Categorization of Responding Installations for the Rich and Remote Variables, by Service 28

4.1 Average Annual Cost Per Child and Maximum Caregiver-to-Child Ratios in CDC Care, by Child Age 38

4.2 Average Annual Cost Per Child in CDC Care, by Child Age and Service 40

4.3 Average Other Costs and Food Costs Per Child for CDC Care, by Service 40

4.4 Average Number of Children in CDC Care at an Installation, by Child Age and Service 41

4.5 Percentage of Children in Each Age Group in CDC Care, by Service 42

4.6 Average Center Size, by Service 42

4.7 Average Annual Cost Per Child in FCC, by Child Age 46

4.8 Average Annual Cost Per Child in FCC, by Service .. 47

4.9 Median Percentage of Children in Each Age Group in FCC, by Service 48

4.10 Provision of FCC Subsidies: Number of Subsidies by Child Age and Service 49

4.11   Median FCC Subsidy Per Week, by Child Age, at
       Installations Providing a Subsidy 50
4.12   Median Percentage of a Provider's Own Children
       Served in FCC, by Service 51
4.13   Percentage of Average Costs Covered by Category III
       Parent Fee, by Child Age 52
4.14   NAF Expenditures as a Percentage of Total Child-
       Development Program Expenditures 53
4.15   Characteristics of Contractor-Operated Centers   . . . 55
4.16   Estimated Cost Per Child in Contractor-Operated
       Centers   58
 5.1   Characteristics of Sponsoring Employers   63
 5.2   Characteristics of Visited Centers 65
 B.1   Analysis of Cost per Infant 117
 B.2   Analysis of Cost per Pre-toddler 117
 B.3   Analysis of Cost per Toddler   118
 B.4   Analysis of Cost per Preschooler   118
 B.5   Analysis of Other Costs per Child 120
 B.6   Analysis of Food Cost per Child 120
 B.7   Analysis of Direct-Care Labor Cost per Infant 121

The Department of Defense (DoD) has developed an impressive system for delivering quality child care to the children of DoD employees. This system currently provides care to nearly 200,000 children on a daily basis, ranging in age from six weeks to 12 years. To care for these children, the DoD operates Child Development Centers (CDCs) around the world, supports a network of Family Child Care (FCC) homes, and offers before- and after-school, holiday, and summer programs for school-age children.

The military child-care system is the largest system of employer-sponsored child care in the country, and it has received wide recognition for the high-quality and affordable care it provides. At the same time, the DoD has been under pressure to control expenditures and has explored how the cost of support activities such as child care might be reduced. In the mid-1990s, part of this examination included discussions on the feasibility and potential value of outsourcing military child care. Although the impetus to outsource has waned as policymakers realized that there were limited opportunities for cost savings through outsourcing of child care, given the strict staffing requirements in the delivery of high-quality care, information about the cost of child care remains an important management and policy tool.

As policymakers consider the various options for providing child care for DoD employees, detailed information regarding the cost of providing such care can help in formulating policy designed to provide an optimal mix of care options.

STUDY PURPOSE

The objective of this study is to develop estimates of the costs associated with providing care in DoD-operated CDCs, in FCCs,[1] in school-age care (SAC) operated by Child Development Programs (CDPs), and in centers operated by outside providers under contract to the DoD. Separate child-care cost estimates were made for children of different ages, even though a long-standing DoD policy bases CDC parent fees[2] on total family income rather than on the age of the children in care.

This report is designed to assist the DoD and Service policymakers in assessing the trade-offs associated with alternative arrangements and in creating policies that optimize the mix of care options given child-care policy goals. A secondary purpose of this work is to place DoD-sponsored child care in the context of employer-sponsored care provided by other government agencies and private employers.

This report provides, for the first time, an analysis of child-care costs across all the Services. A U.S. General Accounting Office (GAO) report examined military child-care costs but focused exclusively on the Air Force (GAO, 1999). Service reports on child care provide some cost information, but those reports generally focus on appropriated funds (government) expenditures, and they report only on costs for a single slot[3] averaged across child age.

SCOPE OF THE STUDY

We examined the combined amount that parents and the DoD spend to provide child care for DoD children. We report cost estimates

---

[1]Family Child Care is provided by military spouses within their government housing. Recently, some FCCs have been authorized to operate outside a military installation. FCC is part of the Child Development System (CDS) and is overseen by CDS employees. The care providers are not military employees but are independent workers providing a service that must conform to government rules.

[2]Parent fees are paid out of pocket. A fee policy determines the amount of the payment, which is based on total family income. Parent fees are distinguished from child-care costs, which include parent fees plus amount spent by the DoD for delivering child care.

[3]A "slot" is a full-time-equivalent space that may be used by a single child or shared by multiple children, depending on how the center or FCC operates.

across Services and across the age ranges served in CDCs and in FCC. The analyses and findings presented in this report are based on the data collected for this study. The primary cost data were obtained from a self-administered survey mailed in late 1999 to CDP managers at a representative sample of 69 DoD installations across the Services and to managers of contractor-operated centers that serve DoD children. These data are limited to DoD child-care provision sponsored by CDPs. Only those school-age care programs operated by CDPs (often in CDCs) are included in our analyses. Child care sponsored by Youth Programs, which sponsor the vast majority of programs for school-aged children (including before- and after-school, summer, and holiday programs), are not included. Our estimates of cost per school-aged-care slot should be interpreted accordingly.

In addition to the cost survey and analysis, we gathered information, including cost data, on employer-sponsored care provided by a small number of civilian employers. We visited seven employer-sponsored child-care centers in the civilian sector. The purpose of the visits was to provide insights on how civilian employers assume and manage child-care costs.

We did not attempt to identify cost drivers or best practices, which are key components of full-blown cost studies. To conduct a cost study that comprehensive, we would have had to substantially increase the burden on our respondents. We did, however, collect the data necessary to single out the installations that operate most effectively. If it is of interest to better understand the practices that enable some installations to deliver child care more efficiently than others, further work may involve revisiting those installations to determine how those best practices contribute to delivering child care at a lower cost.

FINDINGS

Our findings are divided into two general categories—findings on care provided in DoD-operated and contractor-operated centers, and findings on care provided in DoD-licensed FCC homes.

Center-Based Care

Our analyses generated cost estimates for DoD-run center-based care that were similar to estimates generated by the GAO in a recent study of Air Force CDCs (GAO, 1999). The cost of caring for children in the youngest age group (infants) is highest, and the cost per child decreases with successively older age groups (see Chapter Four for a definition of the various age groups). In center-based care, the estimated cost per infant is approximately three times higher than the cost per school-age child. Because the DoD parent fee policy does not depend on the age of the child, we find that, on average, parent fees cover a small proportion (only 29 percent) of center-based infant care. The percentage of total costs covered by parent fees increases with the age of the child, to the point at which parent fees cover 76 percent of the cost of school-age care.

We found substantial variation across installations in the cost per slot of providing care in CDCs. Our analyses revealed that installations with larger CDCs have lower per-child costs. Our analyses also reveal that it costs more to provide care on installations located in areas with a high cost of living, and it costs less to provide care on installations located in areas with a low cost of living. Our analyses revealed weak evidence of differences across Services in the cost per child of CDC care. After controlling for other factors, such as average center size and cost of living, our analyses suggest that costs at Navy and Air Force installations are higher than costs at Marine Corps installations, but the statistical significance of those results is relatively weak. The remoteness[4] of an installation and mix of age groups cared for on an installation did not have a significant relationship to the per-child cost by age group.

While we surveyed all contractor-operated centers serving DoD employees located on DoD installations, this data source was limited because there are few such centers. The information we did gather provided no evidence that contractor-operated centers reduce costs for parents or the DoD. Although the costs of care for young children (infants and pre-toddlers) appear to be lower in these centers, young

---

[4]Remote installations were identified by combining information about population density in an installation's local area with information on the distance to the nearest city. Chapter Three contains a discussion on remote installations.

children make up a small portion of all the children served in them. On the other hand, the cost of care for older children appears to be about the same or even higher in contractor-operated centers than in DoD-run CDCs.

Although our analyses indicate that providing high-quality center-based care is costly, our site visits to civilian employer-sponsored child-care centers suggest that DoD child care is more cost efficient than the care provided by the private employers we studied. These site visits also revealed that employers face stark trade-offs in balancing quality, accessibility, and cost. Many employers choose to make very high-quality care available at a highly subsidized rate to a very small percentage of employees. We observed no employer providing high-quality low-cost care to a large proportion of employees, as the DoD does routinely.

Family Child Care

We also gathered data on the per-child cost of care provided in DoD-licensed FCC homes. We found the cost of FCC care to be substantially lower than the cost of center-based care, particularly for the youngest children. Per-child cost in FCC homes did not vary dramatically by Service or across children's ages.

CONCLUSIONS AND RECOMMENDATIONS

Child care is a costly benefit and the costs are even higher for younger children. At the same time, the incremental cost of high-quality care over mediocre or poor-quality care is quite small. What we know about the benefits of high-quality care to children suggests that providing high-quality care is a very good investment, particularly in light of the small incremental cost involved.

Care provided in centers is particularly costly. Our analyses revealed that costs across centers vary substantially while also highlighting some cost differences across the Military Services. We did not observe a consistent difference between the cost of contractor-operated centers versus the cost of DoD-operated centers. Cost differences across centers appear to be significantly influenced by the number of children being served at a given center, with lower per-child costs in larger centers. CDC costs are also influenced by the cost of living in the local area, with higher per-child costs observed at installations located in areas with a higher cost of living.

Our survey of the care centers revealed dramatic differences across installations in the cost of care per child. While some of the variation reflects idiosyncratic differences in expenditures (for example, one center went through a major renovation and all the costs of the renovation were incurred in the study year), much of the variation is not explainable by such factors. An examination of this variation represents a useful opportunity for DoD CDCs to learn from one another and potentially identify opportunities to reduce costs without sacrificing quality.

Our data indicate that the cost of care in FCC is considerably lower than the cost of CDC care. Cost is not so closely tied to a child's age in FCC; consequently, cost savings for the youngest children are the most substantial. However, cost comparisons with CDCs must be made with certain reservations.

Our analyses revealed that the cost of contractor-operated centers clearly falls within the range of costs observed for DoD-run centers. The cost per infant in the contractor-operated centers is generally lower than the cost per infant in DoD-run centers, whereas the cost per preschooler in the contractor-operated centers is generally higher than the cost per preschooler in DoD-run centers. There is, therefore, no evidence that contractor-run centers are 10-percent cheaper to run than DoD-run centers, which is a DoD requirement for outsourcing.

We urge the DoD to use the cost data provided in this report in concert with clearly articulated child-care system goals to develop policy that will produce an optimal mix of child-care options. It is clear, for example, that FCC care, particularly for infants, is cost-efficient. A more aggressive subsidy policy, as well as other approaches that the Services are currently pursuing, could increase the attractiveness of this option to both parents and providers. Our data also indicate that CDC size is an important cost driver. The DoD may want to develop policy that encourages larger and more cost-effective CDCs.

Military child care provides high-quality care to high numbers of children. Generous subsidies enable this care to be affordable as well. With the cost data provided in this report, the DoD has an additional tool at its disposal that can help it to improve system efficiency while maintaining the quality, affordability, and reach that make military child care a model for the nation.

ACKNOWLEDGMENTS

This report benefited from the contributions of a number of people. We would like to thank our hosts at our pretest sites—Brian Floyd, Deborah Singleton, Camie Carlson, and Sandy Berry—all of whom were extremely cooperative and helpful. They not only completed the survey form as best they could, but they also clocked their progress and talked at length with us about the complexities and problems the surveys had presented. Thanks to these people, we were able to modify and simplify the survey.

Our RAND colleague Richard Buddin provided his database and expertise; we used both to help draw the sample. Jorge Munoz, Sandy Chien, Nicole Humphrey, Chris Fair, and Joy Moini provided crucial research support. We would also like to thank our reviewers, Rebecca Kilburn, Linda Smith, and Ron Zimmer, who provided many insightful comments and suggestions on an earlier draft that much improved this report. Lisa Hochman and Donna White provided secretarial support through the various stages of this project, and Nancy DelFavero edited the final report.

We very much appreciate the constructive comments of the Service Child Care Managers, Dr. Beverly Schmalzried, M. A. Lucas, Pam Crespi, and Michael Berger, as well as Richard Fullerton and the participants at the 2001 Western Economic Association Conference. Jan Witte and Barbara Thompson of the Office of Children and Youth were always willing to provide data and advice, as was Carolee VanHorn before she left that office. Madeline Fried of Fried and Sher provided us with a list of civilian centers identified by *Working Mother* magazine that they had aggregated with additional descriptive information, which helped us to select civilian employee-sponsored centers to visit.

AGI	Adjusted gross income
APF	Appropriated funds
CCDBG	Child Care and Development Block Grant
CDC	Child Development Center
CDF	Children's Defense Fund
CDP	Child Development Program
CDS	Child Development System
DHHS	U.S. Department of Health and Human Services
DLA	Defense Logistics Agency
DoD	Department of Defense
DoDI	Department of Defense Instruction
FCC	Family Child Care
FTE	Full-time equivalent
FY	Fiscal year
GAO	General Accounting Office
GS	Government service
GSA	General Services Administration

HR	Human resources
MCCA	Military Child Care Act
MEO	Most Efficient Organization
NAEYC	National Association for the Education of Young Children
NAF	Nonappropriated funds
NAFCC	National Association of Family Child Care
NAVICP	Naval Inventory Control Point
NSA	National Security Agency
NSACA	National School-Age Care Alliance
OMB	Office of Management and Budget
PCS	Permanent Change of Station
PWS	Performance Work Statement
RFP	Request for proposal
SAC	School-age care
SMSA	Standard Metropolitan Statistical Area
TANF	Temporary Assistance to Needy Families
USDA	United States Department of Agriculture

Chapter One

INTRODUCTION

As the percentage of dual working parents with young children increases, the need for child care increases as well. Most of this care is provided informally, either by a parent who is off work (when each parent works different shifts), by a parent while he or she is working, or by a child's sibling or other relative. In recent years, however, increasing numbers of young children are entering more-formal care provided by licensed family-care networks or child-care centers.[1] Much of this formal care is delivered by the nonprofit sector through programs in churches and synagogues, community centers, and, increasingly, schools.

However, as the need for care has continued to increase, for-profit firms have become more prominent in delivering child care. Of the more than nine million children under the age of five in nonrelative-provided child care in 1995, almost six million were enrolled in organized facilities, day care centers, nurseries or preschools, Head

---

[1]The increased use of formal child care also reflects the diminished availability of extended family members, upon whom young parents could count in times past for free or very inexpensive care. Welfare reform, in particular, with its emphasis on getting women with young children out of the home and into the workforce, has reduced the number of friends, relatives, and neighbors available to care for one's children. Moreover, in some states (for example, California), Temporary Assistance to Needy Families (TANF) programs changed the way that providers are paid. Child-care subsidy funds that in the past were provided to parents, who then paid the providers themselves, are now paid directly to providers by TANF program administrators or their representatives (in California, Alternative Payment Providers). To receive these direct payments, providers may not live in the recipient household and must have a social security number, something that many women in immigrant communities do not possess and cannot obtain because of their resident status.

Start, or school programs (Smith, 2000). Although parents are increasingly turning to formal child-care options, consensus is strong that the quality of much of the civilian care for young children that is available today in this country is mediocre at best (Cost, Quality, and Child Outcomes Study Team, 1995; GAO, 1999; Campbell et al., 2000).

Partly in response to the limited options for high-quality care, over the past decade or so increasing numbers of employers around the country have made the decision to provide worksite child-care centers.[2] For example, in 1982, the National Employer-Supported Child Care Project identified 204 worksite facilities in the United States; as of 1996, 1,800 such facilities were identified. For the most part, these centers are of small to medium size.[3] Burud and Associates (1996) report the average capacity of the centers in their study was 105 children. Hence, they serve only a trivial number of children and an even smaller number of families, as most of these centers make care available to siblings of enrolled children on a priority basis.

The U.S. military represents a notable exception to the usual situation in employer-sponsored child care—a small number of slots in a limited number of sites. The military today provides care to about 200,000 children from 6 weeks to 12 years of age in more than 800 Child Development Centers (CDCs) around the world, in more than 9,000 Family Child Care (FCC) homes,[4] and in before- and after-school and holiday and summer programs.[5] Indeed, the military is the largest provider by far of employer-sponsored care in this country. In contrast to most civilian employers, the military is quite concerned about meeting a large share of employee need for care. Indeed, the military has developed a formula to assess need at each installation that enables it to assess the degree to which available

---

[2]Employers believe that worksite child-care centers increase staff loyalty and improve recruiting and retention.

[3]Military child care was not included in the project study.

[4]The Navy uses a different term to describe FCC: "child development homes."

[5]Because some spaces are shared, the 169,972 available spaces serve a number of children even higher than that (DoD, 2000).

care is meeting overall need.[6] Currently, the military child development system provides 169,972 spaces, and has committed itself to ultimately providing 215,112 spaces (or slots) by fiscal year 2007. Calculated by slot, the military has estimated the potential need to be 268,890 slots.

As discussed in the next chapter, the military child-care system has received much praise for its quality. At the same time, in an era of defense budget cuts, intense scrutiny has been placed on the cost of support activities, such as child care, that are not central to the Department of Defense's (DoD's) core mission.

THE LINK BETWEEN COST AND QUALITY

Child care is a highly labor-intensive operation, with labor costs accounting for the greatest share of costs.[7] The quality of child care is typically evaluated across many dimensions; however, the staff-child ratio and size of the group or classroom are important features of any examination of child-care quality.[8] Such a definition of quality implies that, all other things being equal, it is more costly to provide high-quality than low-quality care. The costs of providing high-

---

[6]The formula uses information on the family characteristics of military personnel and on the total number of civilians working at the installation to estimate the need for child care at the installation. The estimate of the number of slots needed by military personnel is based on installation-level personnel information on the number of children age 0–5 and 6–12, marital status of military personnel, and employment status of spouses. The DoD feeds this information into a formula that reflects the fact that families with different characteristics will have different probabilities of using DoD child care—either because the children do not live with their parents, because the spouse does not work outside the home, or because the family makes other arrangements. For example, the formula assumes, based on DoD experience, that the children of single parents or two active duty military parents are more likely to require child care than children with a civilian parent who works only part time. The estimate of the number of slots required by civilians is based on the total number of civilians working at the installations. The military and civilian estimates are combined to produce the number of slots needed by each installation. These numbers are then summed for the DoD as a whole.

[7]A recent U.S. General Accounting Office report found that labor costs account for 75 percent of the total cost of providing child care in the Air Force (GAO, 1999). Culkin, Morris, and Helburn (1991) examined the cost of care at seven centers and found that labor costs account for between 56 and 72 percent of costs at those centers.

[8]See Cost, Quality, and Child Outcomes Study Team (1995) for a summary of several instruments used to evaluate the quality of child care.

quality care must be paid by someone—parents, employers, governments, or charity groups—and some argue that a lack of resources is an important reason for the overall low quality of care (Schulman, 2000).

The full cost of high-quality care is substantial—well beyond the means of most parents (Schulman, 2000). For example, the U.S. General Accounting Office (GAO) report found that in Air Force Child Development Centers the cost per child-hour for infants (who are, because of the need for very low child-to-staff ratios, the most expensive children for whom to provide care) was $5.43 per hour. Per-hour costs averaged across all child age groups were $3.86 per child-hour.[9]

Unless the cost of care is subsidized by the government, a philanthropic agency, or an employer, high costs translate into high parent fees. Although the cost of care is prohibitively high for some parents, several researchers have noted that low wages[10] paid to child-care workers represent another subsidy to parents (Campbell et al., 2000; Cost, Quality, and Child Outcomes Study Team, 1995). If not for this "subsidy," child-care fees would be even higher.

There are a number of government programs that provide assistance to families in meeting their child-care expenses. The federal government offers a Child Care Tax Credit.[11] The states provide a variety of forms of child-care assistance, including, in more than 40 states, state-funded pre-kindergarten programs. The Child Care and

---

[9]The GAO study calculated the production cost, or how much the CDCs spent in producing an hour of care. This cost is covered by a combination of parent fees and DoD funding.

[10]The Cost Quality and Child Outcomes Study Team (1995) found that the average child-care worker would require a 45 percent raise to achieve wage parity with the average worker of the same gender, education, age, and minority status in the economy as a whole.

[11]The Child Care Tax Credit is available to some individuals paying for child care for dependents age 13 and younger. To qualify, the child or children must be living with those receiving the credit and the child care must be used to enable the credit recipient to work or conduct a job search. The credit represents a percentage of adjusted gross income (AGI) ranging from 20 to 30 percent, with the lower percentage rates applied to higher incomes. The maximum credit is $2,400 for one child and $4,800 for two or more children. Any employer-provided benefits must be subtracted from the calculated tax credit.

Development Block Grant (CCDBG) provides funds to states to subsidize child care for low-income families through both grants to providers and vouchers to parents. The Temporary Assistance to Needy Families (TANF) program provides funds to states to subsidize child-care costs for women who must enter training or employment as a condition of receiving their welfare grant. Because of limited funds and strict income limits on most of these subsidies, these programs serve only a fraction of families that need assistance. For example, the CCDBG reaches only 12 percent of children eligible under federal guidelines (Campbell et al., 2000; DHHS, 1999). As a result, a large percentage of working families must cover the cost of child care without assistance. Many spend well over the 10 percent of gross income that experts recommend be allocated to child care (Schulman, 2000).

While cost is the major reason for low-quality care, difficulties in assessing quality care are also contributing factors. Most people can't distinguish high-quality care from low-quality care when they see it, so they cannot make an informed choice concerning quality even if they are motivated to do so (Cost, Quality, and Child Outcomes Study Team, 1995). It has been asserted that even those parents who might be able to afford high-quality care lack the knowledge necessary to assess what constitutes high-quality care. Therefore, they may wind up inadvertently paying for high-quality care but receiving care of a lesser quality (Price, 2000; Cost Quality and Child Outcomes Study Team, 1995).

THE ROLE OF QUALITY STANDARDS IN CARE DELIVERY

A number of mechanisms and standards have been created to support the delivery of higher-quality care. State licensing represents one mechanism through which quality is supported and enforced. However, existing state licensing operations generally focus on easily accessible and measurable criteria, such as square footage and the presence of safety gates at child-care facilities. While such attributes are indeed critical to ensuring young children's well-being and safety, they do not address the quality of the relationship between children and caregivers, which is the aspect of quality more closely linked to developmental outcomes (Belsky, 1984; Bredekamp, 1986).

About half the states now offer some additional reimbursement to child-care providers who serve low-income families. Using tiered reimbursement based on provider characteristics, states provide additional funds to accredited providers, those that require specified staff training, and those that offer child-to-staff ratios that are lower than those required for licensing, among other features (Blank, Behr, and Schulman, 2000).

Accreditation by the National Association for the Education of Young Children (NAEYC) is a voluntary process that holds centers to a higher quality standard. To become accredited, a center must engage in a three-step process that includes self-study, a site validation visit, and a commission decision.[12] The process must be repeated every three years. An accreditation process is available for family-based care through the National Association of Family Child Care (NAFCC) and for school-age care through the National School-Age Care Alliance (NSACA).

Zellman, Johansen, and Van Winkle (1994, pp. 35–36) compared DoD certification standards and NAEYC accreditation requirements to illustrate the differences between certification and accreditation:

> Comparisons of the two sets of standards on environment and curriculum help to illustrate the qualitative differences between certification and accreditation. Certification and accreditation have identical standards for minimum usable indoor and outdoor play areas. NAEYC (the accrediting body), however, provides specifics on room layout, storage areas, the provision of cushions and carpeted areas, and the variety of surfaces that should be incorporated into the playground. Both sets of requirements stress a developmentally appropriate curriculum, but NAEYC's program descriptions are much more extensive and include types of activities, a mix of activities, and the presentation of multicultural learning opportunities. . . . Another important difference between accreditation and certification is the relative emphasis on caregiver relationships with children. Certification checks that caregivers respond appropriately to children, but the certification checklist lacks any definition or standard for appropriateness . . . it is assumed that appropriate behavior will follow from the training, although the

---

[12]See NAEYC (1991) for more details on the accreditation process.

nature of that behavior is not explicitly stated in the certification criteria.

Welfare reform initiatives represent another opportunity for government to exert pressure on providers to improve the quality of care. Enormous amounts of public funds currently are being spent to provide care for the children of welfare recipients who, under the TANF legislation, are required to participate in training or employment as a condition of continuing to receive welfare support.[13] Many states have responded to the resulting enormous need for child care by funding whatever care parents can find for their children. California is a typical case. The state has adopted a "parental choice" plan, which allows parents complete freedom to select care, including unlicensed care, for their children. Viewing TANF primarily as an employment program, the state did not choose to use these funds as a lever to improve child-care quality. This leverage could have been exerted in a number of ways. For example, the state could have required that all care be licensed.[14]

Although government regulation and high quality standards appear at first glance to be an effective way of increasing the overall quality of care, Chipty (1995) found that many day care providers meet, but do not exceed, state licensing standards. One reason that providers may not exceed minimal standards is that higher standards increase the cost of care. When costs increase, providers have two unattractive options: absorb the additional cost or raise the price. When prices increase, parents generally purchase less care. Either way, Chipty contends, providers don't benefit financially from providing higher-quality care.[15]

---

[13]The Child Care and Development Fund, created by the Personal Responsibility and Work Opportunity Reconciliation Act of 1996, provided a total of $4.6 billion for child-care programs in fiscal year 2001.

[14]One reason states chose not to create quality criteria was that they wanted to maximize the number of available slots so that more women could work or enter training. Tying funding to license status or other quality indicators reduces the number of slots that are available, at least in the near term.

[15]The market dynamics described by Chipty do not apply in DoD CDCs, where care is heavily subsidized and standards far exceed minimal licensing requirements.

REDUCING COSTS WITHOUT REDUCING QUALITY

As we noted earlier, child care is a labor-intensive activity, and high-quality care requires more labor than low-quality care. Within this reality, many observers have speculated about ways to provide high-quality care in a more cost-effective manner, including relying on nonprofits, receipt of government support, and promoting larger centers. Mocan (1997), for example, finds that despite widespread support for nonprofit centers, they are no more or no less efficient at providing child care, holding the quality levels constant.[16] He has also found that centers that receive public money (state or federal) that is tied to higher standards have variable costs that are 25 percent higher than other centers. Mocan also finds some evidence that larger centers are more efficient (due to economies of scale), as are centers that serve children of different ages (due to economies of scope).

In the past five years, the DoD has considered the extent to which competitive sourcing of DoD CDCs will reduce costs. Any serious evaluation of this policy needs to be informed by solid data on child-care costs and must be based on an understanding of the potential sources of savings. These data would be helpful even if child care continued to be operated by the military; such cost data might help in determining appropriate center sizes and in thinking through the relative magnitude and scope of the different system components. The need for these data led the DoD to ask RAND to investigate the cost of delivering military child care. Unlike the GAO report mentioned earlier, the RAND mandate included all the Military Services and extended the scope of the effort beyond CDCs to FCC and school-age care (SAC).[17] And unlike the GAO report, RAND also investigated the delivery of child care in the worksite by DoD contractors and by civilian employers in order to contextualize the results of the work and draw more meaningful implications for policymakers, practitioners, and employers.

---

[16]This finding is consistent with Mukerjee and White (1993).

[17]Our analysis of school-age care costs had to be limited to school-age care provided in CDCs since our survey went to CDC staff. The proportion of school-age care in CDCs is on the decline as services have attempted to increase the number of preschool slots by moving school-age care out of CDCs.

In Chapter Two of this report, we provide an overview of the military child-care system. In Chapters Three and Four, we present the methods and results of a cost survey of military CDCs. Next, in Chapter Five, we present the results of our visits to a number of centers supported by civilian employers, including the federal General Services Administration (GSA). In Chapter Six, we conclude with a discussion of the implications of our findings for military and civilian child care.

Chapter Two

AN OVERVIEW OF THE MILITARY CHILD-CARE SYSTEM

The system of care that the military has established has been a subject of considerable interest not only among policymakers and researchers, but also among other employers who are considering whether to provide child care for their employees. Interest in the DoD child-care system stems not only from its enormous size and complexity, but also the multiple indicators of its quality, particularly its rate of NAEYC accreditation, which far exceeds that for civilian child-care centers. Today, the accreditation rate in military CDCs is 96 percent; the equivalent rate in the civilian sector is only 8 percent (Campbell et al., 2000, p. 15).[1]

The large scale of military child care reflects an enormous workforce with unique child-care needs. It is understood, for example, that the frequent Permanent Change of Station (PCS) moves that personnel must make reduce the likelihood that such personnel can access child care from extended family members. Having work hours that may extend well beyond the normal workday presents an added challenge. Dual military families in particular may need care at non-standard times. The scope of the military's response reflects this substantial need. Indeed, military planners were asked to develop a method that would enable the DoD child-care system to assess need and meet more of that need over time. The ultimate goal is to provide

---

[1]To be eligible for first-time accreditation, a center must have operated for at least one year. For renewals, a center can be granted a deferral if there has been a change in directorship or the center has undertaken a major construction project.

215,112 spaces (or slots) by fiscal year 2007. Need is established through a DoD formula that considers key indicators such as the number of children living on a given installation under the age of five.

Military child care is provided as part of a system of care designed to meet children's needs as they age, so that children can be served by the child-care system practically from birth until age 12. A variety of venues enable the system to meet parents' needs for reliable care while recognizing parental preferences concerning the nature of the care environment. Consequently, the military provides care for as much as 12 hours a day in CDCs and even longer, if necessary, in FCC homes. For those with more-limited needs, the system can also be used on a part-time or hourly basis in many locations.

The military has had a complex relationship with FCC. Because FCC generally takes place in government living quarters, it is far less observable than CDC care.[2] For this reason, commanders in the days prior to the Military Child Care Act (MCCA) of 1989 often had qualms about FCC that were shared by many parents. Contributing to its stepchild status was the almost total absence, in those early days, of any regulation. Although the military was regulating FCC to some degree as early as 1983, during RAND's first study of military child care, interviewees frequently viewed FCC primarily as a spouse-employment program. According to one respondent, the FCC was an opportunity "for military wives to make some money while being able to be with their own young children" (Zellman et al., 1992). A person providing FCC was likened by more than one interviewee to an "Avon lady": Providing FCC was a business that a military spouse could run out of her home. Said one respondent in that early study, "We don't regulate the Avon lady or tell her how much or what kind of lipstick to sell. So we can't do that with [family child care], either" (Zellman et al., 1992).

In that same study, Zellman et al. note a number of positive attributes associated with FCC that the military might want to exploit as it proceeded to build a military child-care system. Those attributes included the ability to care for children for extended periods

---

[2]FCC can occur off base. There, it operates under a Memorandum of Understanding with the state, and the provider is licensed by the service.

(including nights and weekends), to keep mildly ill children in care, and to fairly readily increase or decrease the number of available slots based on need. Finally, FCC promised to expand the capacity of the growing military child-care system without the need to invest in costly CDCs, which required years to design and build.

The military moved swiftly to institute a number of reforms to FCC. Key was the DoD's decision to apply to FCC most of the requirements in the MCCA of 1989, which focused only on CDCs. The decision to apply MCCA standards to the operation of FCC signaled the military's decisive step away from equating FCC with the selling of cosmetics. Now, FCC providers are expected to undergo training and are subject to the same no-notice inspections as are CDCs.

However, limited use of subsidies for FCC has given a distorted picture of the value of FCC as part of the military child-care system. Previous work has identified a strong preference among parents for CDC care over FCC (Macro International, Inc., 1999, and Zellman et al., 1992). That preference can be partly attributed to the attractive CDCs that have been built in recent years, partly to fears about the isolation of and lack of day-to-day oversight in FCC, and partly to the inherently lower level of dependability that an individual can provide as compared with an institution. But the preference for CDC care can also partly be traced to the fact that for parents in the lower fee categories, the inherently less-attractive child-care alternative of FCC costs even more when no subsidy is provided.

To a limited degree, the Services have addressed the FCC cost problem through the use of subsidies. The DoD has authorized subsidies to FCC providers, which are being used to further specific goals, such as increased infant slots, extended-hours care, and care for children with special needs. When an FCC provider claims a subsidy, the provider must agree to set his or her fees at the same level as the CDC fees. Such a policy obviously benefits parents and removes a disincentive to use FCC. Subsidies are discussed in more detail in Chapter Four.

It is the quality of care that is provided that has brought the most attention to the military child-care system. The high quality of this care is largely a function of the MCCA of 1989. This act was written and passed in response to concerns about the quality of military child care, and was precipitated by several incidents of child abuse in military centers. The MCCA sought to improve the quantity and quality of child care provided on military installations. An additional aim of the act was to standardize the delivery, quality, and cost of care across installations and Military Services, which in 1989 varied considerably. The MCCA relied on four policies to realize the goals of the legislation: (1) substantial pay increases for those who worked directly with children, with pay raises tied to the completion of training milestones; (2) the hiring of a training and curriculum specialist in each CDC to direct and oversee staff training and curriculum development;[3] (3) the requirement that parent fees (based on total family income) be at least matched, dollar for dollar, with appropriated (government) funds; and (4) the institution of unannounced inspections of CDCs to be conducted four times yearly.[4]

An additional goal for the framers of the MCCA was to ensure that child-care costs would not absorb too much of a family's resources. This was a particular concern for young families, who tend to have both the smallest incomes and the youngest children. Because staff-to-child ratios are tied to child age, the cost of providing care to very young children is substantially higher than the cost of care for older children. If parents were assessed fees based on child-care costs, the youngest, lowest-income parents would be paying the most. These higher fees would then represent a much larger percentage of their income. For these reasons, the decision was made to not tie CDC fees to child age but rather to base them on total family income. The idea was that if children use CDC care from age zero to five, parent fees cover an increasing portion of the cost of care over time.

The military's fee structure groups families into five fee categories based on total family income. As shown in Table 2.1, the distribution of families across fee categories varies by Service; the Air Force and Navy have the highest percentages of families in the highest fee cate-

---

[3]It was believed that a training and curriculum specialist in each CDC would be an important contributor to high-quality care. The framers of the MCCA rejected the idea of regionalizing this function, which is frequently done by for-profit providers (see Chapter Five for further discussion of this function in civilian centers).

[4]The appropriated-funds match of parent fees, plus provision of the CDC building and its maintenance, ensures that the subsidy for CDC care is more than 50 percent.

Table 2.1

Summary of FY 1998 to 1999 DoD Child-Care Fee Report

Income Category	Army		Navy		Marine Corps		Air Force		DoD	
	Percentage of Families in Category	Average Weekly Child-Care Fee	Percentage of Families in Category	Average Weekly Child-Care Fee	Percentage of Families in Category	Average Weekly Child-Care Fee	Percentage of Families in Category	Average Weekly Child-Care Fee	Percentage of Families in Category	Average Weekly Child-Care Fee
I: $0–$23,000	14%	$47	11%	$48	11%	$50	9%	$49	11%	$49
II: $23,001–$34,000	31%	$57	29%	$58	35%	$60	28%	$59	30%	$59
III: $34,001–$44,000	21%	$69	20%	$71	22%	$71	21%	$71	21%	$70
IV: $44,001–$55,000	16%	$82	19%	$81	16%	$81	22%	$81	18%	$81
V: $55,001+	19%	$94	21%	$93	16%	$93	21%	$92	19%	$93

NOTE: The income categories shown here are based on FY 1998 to 1999 fee structure data. In FY 1999 to 2000, a sixth category was added, which is not shown here. The information in this table was obtained from materials provided by the DoD Office of Family Policy. Totals may not add to 100 percent.

gory; the Army has the highest percentage of families in the lowest fee category.

The average weekly child-care fee in the time frame covered by this report was $70. Assuming 50 weeks of care a year, this figure is well below the yearly $4,000 to $6,000 that the Children's Defense Fund (CDF) Report (Schulman, 2000) found to be the average cost for care for a four-year-old. Civilian care for a younger child would be even more; the CDF report found that center care for infants is on average $1,100 higher per year than the cost of center care for a four-year-old.

The requirements of the MCCA were, however, largely limited to center-based care; the DoD was not required to do much of anything with FCC or SAC. However, the DoD realized that if it met only MCCA requirements it would wind up with much-improved centers whose quality would contrast dramatically with that found in FCC and SAC. This, in turn, would increase parental demand for center care, a much more costly alternative. So, the DoD decided to apply the MCCA's quality initiatives to all three settings. As a consequence of this decision, the military runs a system that provides consistently high-quality care. Nearly all CDC care is accredited by the NAEYC; accreditation of FCC and SAC is currently being pursued. For example, nearly all Air Force SAC programs are accredited by the NSACA. (See Zellman and Johansen, 1995, and Campbell et al., 2000, for further discussion of the MCCA.) Indeed, both the Congress and the White House have noted the high quality of the military's Child Development Program (CDP) and have recommended it as a model program for the nation.

How applicable the military model might be to the civilian sector depends heavily on issues of cost. The GAO investigated the costs of military child care and compared them to the costs for civilian centers. The resulting GAO report, issued in October 1999, was limited to Air Force CDCs and compared their costs to available data on civilian centers from the Cost, Quality, and Child Outcomes in Child Care Centers study (1995) conducted by researchers at the University of Colorado at Denver. The study's bottom line was that the cost of high-quality care in Air Force and civilian centers were not substantially different. The adjusted Air Force cost per child-hour was $3.42, which is about 7 percent higher than the cost of care in civilian centers.[5] Much of this differential can be explained by the fact that Air Force centers pay their caregivers, on average, about $1.04 more per hour. The GAO report concludes that high-quality center-based care costs only a little more than other center-based care.

Concurrent with its interest in the cost of quality child care, the DoD considered the possible benefits of outsourcing child-care provision to non-DoD organizations.[6] This exploration coincided with a much larger interest in competitive sourcing and outsourcing in the military that was finding favor at the time (see, for example, Gates and Robbert, 2000; Pint and Baldwin, 1997; and Robbert, Gates, and Elliott, 1997).[7] The general argument behind outsourcing is that organizations have limited senior managerial time and financial resources to invest; organizations should therefore focus their efforts on those activities that can be most effectively managed internally. A general movement away from diversification in the civilian sector has led firms to focus on core competencies—activities central to the organization's mission—in which the organization excels relative to its competitors (Pint and Baldwin, 1997). Outsourcing of the many services that the military provides presumably would allow the

---

[5]The cost per child-hour was $3.86 but was adjusted downward to reflect the differences between Air Force and civilian centers in child age distribution. On average, military centers provide much more care to the youngest children than do civilian centers. The cost of care for the youngest children is the highest because child-to-caregiver ratios are the lowest in groups with the youngest children.

[6]For example, on March 20, 1996, Fred Pang, Assistant Secretary of Defense for Force Management Policy, presented a prepared statement to the Personnel Subcommittee of the Senate Armed Services Committee that noted the following: "We are also conducting two evaluation tests regarding outsourcing child care, recognizing that the department is nearing maximum potential to meet child care needs on base. The first of these tests involves contracting with civilian child care centers in five locations to 'buy down' the cost of spaces for military families to make costs comparable to on-installation care. The second test focuses on outsourcing the management of a defense-owned child care facility in Dayton, Ohio."

[7]It is important to note the distinction between outsourcing and competitive sourcing. The former assumes the work will be contracted out, and the goal is to find the most-efficient external service provider. The latter allows for the possibility that in-house provision of the service may be most efficient. (See Gates and Robbert, 2000, for further discussion of competitive sourcing.)

military to focus on its own core competencies while providing services that could be more flexible, and perhaps less costly as well.[8]

For many in the DoD who were most committed to the idea of outsourcing military services, child care seemed an ideal target. The provision of child care was far from the military's core competencies, and there were firms in the civilian sector that had considerable experience in providing care. The Navy in particular moved forward on this front. In 1996, the Assistant Secretary of the Navy (Manpower and Reserve Affairs), with support from the highest levels of Navy leadership, directed an A-76 study of child-care services for the entire San Diego region.[9] Interestingly, it was the Navy's MEO (Most Efficient Organization) that won the competition in the fall of 1998. The MEO's bid of $43 million over five years represented expected savings of approximately 30 percent over projections based on then-current costs.[10] There were other, more-limited efforts, particularly in military-related organizations, such as the Defense Logistics Agency, to subject child care to the A-76 process.

By 1998, however, the Air Force and the Army had taken the idea of outsourcing child care off the table. The reasons for the Air Force decision included analyses indicating that outsourcing would actually increase costs to both parents and taxpayers, and concern over reduced job opportunities for military spouses (Benken, 1998).

---

[8]The literature on business management emphasizes that cost reduction should not be the primary goal of outsourcing. Improved strategic focus, better performance, and sharing risks with the supplier are all better reasons to make an outsourcing decision (Pint and Baldwin, 1997).

[9]Commercial activities in the DoD are subject to a series of rules and procedures set forth in the U.S. Office of Management and Budget (OMB) Circular A-76. The term "A-76" is often used as shorthand to refer to the rules, procedures, and processes related to the circular. The circular requires all government agencies, including the DoD, to review commercial functions being performed in-house every five years. It also limits the government's ability to directly outsource any activity that currently employs ten or more civil service (but not military) employees by requiring a structured competition that allows the government employees to bid for the work along with other potential private and public sector providers. The government's bid is called the Most Efficient Organization, or MEO. An important step in the competition process is the development of a Performance Work Statement (PWS) that describes, from a customer perspective, the work required. (See Gates and Robbert, 2000, for further details on this process.)

[10]The PWS specified an affordability target of $62 million over five years. Presumably, bids higher than this would have been rejected.

Nevertheless, the push toward outsourcing was a source of consider-able concern to those in the DoD who had worked hard to foster the child-care system and implement the many changes that had moved it from being just mediocre to being outstanding. With growing pres-sure to outsource, it became clear that key information, such as cost per child by child age, had to be readily available in order to make informed decisions about the best way to provide high-quality, cost-effective care.

These somewhat inconsistent views of military child care—on the one hand, an asset to the military and to the whole nation as a model for civilian-sector child care, while, on the other hand, something ancillary to the military's major activities and therefore an activity that potentially should be outsourced—were very much in evidence when we began our work on this study. We revisit these issues fre-quently throughout this report.

Chapter Three

STUDY METHODS

The research described in this report involved a number of different methodologies, including an installation cost survey, visits to civilian employer-sponsored child-care centers, and interviews with human resources (HR) managers who supervise the child-care centers that we visited.

This project was originally motivated by Service-level interest in subjecting DoD child-care activities to competitive sourcing studies. As a result, our examination of cost assumed a perspective that is most relevant for that purpose. Throughout our analyses, we consider *cost* to be the combined amount spent by the DoD and by parents (whom we view as the key consumers of child care) in providing child-care services. This definition of cost, then, reflects the *cost to the consumer*. It is important to note that most studies of child-care cost (for example, those described in Chapter One) attempt to capture the *production cost* of child care—how much the providers spend in providing care—rather than the cost to consumers. Production costs can differ from the cost to consumers for a variety of reasons. If, for example, the provider is a for-profit organization, it might charge consumers more than the actual production cost in order to generate a profit margin. Alternatively, a nonprofit organization might receive donations and therefore charge consumers less than the actual cost of providing the care.

For DoD-run care, the production cost is comparable to the cost to consumers. However, for FCC and contractor-based care, production and consumer costs differ. Because of these differences between production and consumer costs, our cost-estimation techniques necessarily differed for the three types of care (DoD-run CDCs, FCC, and contractor). A discussion of our techniques for estimating costs for each type of care follows.

For DoD-run CDCs, we were able to obtain detailed information on CDC and CDP expenditures. Because the DoD is the provider of child care and the DoD plus parents are the consumers (they jointly pay for the care and reap the benefits of that care), the DoD and the parents form a closed system. Assuming that parent fees are not used for some other purpose, and the CDCs do not receive revenue from sources other than parents and the DoD, the cost estimates we constructed that are based on program expenditures reflect both the cost incurred by the provider in operating the centers *and* the amount paid to the provider by parents and by the DoD (the employer).

In the case of FCC and contractor-operated care, the relationship between production costs and costs to the consumer is more complicated because there is a third party involved. Our cost estimates are based on the amount paid to the provider by the customers (parents plus the DoD) plus any additional cost that the DoD incurs in administering the program. This may not reflect the actual production cost.[1] As stated earlier, production costs might differ from consumer costs for several reasons. For example, a contractor or FCC provider may be earning a profit or incurring a loss, which would not be reflected in our figures. Or, the contractor may have access to additional sources of revenue that are used to support the child-care activity. In addition, the provider may be cross-subsidizing care for children of different age groups (for example, the fees charged for infant care might be less than the full cost of care, while the fees charged for preschool-age children might be more than the actual cost of providing that care).

In examining center and program-level expenditures, we considered both nonappropriated funds (NAF) and appropriated funds (APF) ex-

---

[1]For the contractors included in our study, we were not able to collect data on production costs. In one case, we were unable to do so because the child-care contract was part of a much larger installation-wide contract. With the others, this information was considered proprietary; therefore, we were unable to obtain it. Without this information, we cannot be sure that a "cost estimate" that is limited to the amounts paid by parents and the employer is equal to the cost incurred by the provider.

penditures. APF resources are taxpayer funds appropriated by congress, whereas NAF resources are derived from user fees. Some activities (for example, clubs) at some installations are funded completely by user fees,[2] whereas others, such as child care, are funded through a combination of APF and NAF. In such cases, the DoD pays part of the cost of the activity, and user fees cover the rest. Depending on the activity and the funding formula, NAF can be used for labor or nonlabor expenditures. When employees are paid by NAF, they are not part of competitive civil service. NAF employees are covered by a different set of rules and regulations, and a different pay structure, retirement system, and benefit system. Most DoD CDCs are staffed by a combination of civil service and NAF employees.

According to the MCCA, fees paid by parents for child care must be used to support the CDP and can be used exclusively for funding caregiver wages. Installations may also choose to use the user fees from other activities, such as golf course fees, for child care.[3] As a result, an installation's parent fees should be no greater than, and might be less than, the installation's NAF expenditures on the CDP. Similarly, the fraction of the total child and youth services budget accounted for by parent fees should be less than or equal to APF expenditures as a fraction of total expenditures.

Installations generally did not report expenditures for rent, although they did report repair and maintenance expenses. This phenomenon is not unique to child care. In our experience, DoD agencies account for the cost of space only when they rent space from an outside agency (including the GSA) and pay a monthly rental charge for that space. DoD-owned space is "free" from a cost perspective because the CDP does not pay a monthly rental charge for that space. Contractors often receive "free" space as well. Three of the five contractor-operated child-care centers included in our study received their space directly from the DoD, and the cost of the space did not figure into the contract costs. We learned that such an arrangement

---

[2]Examples of activities funded completely through user fees include bowling alleys, golf courses, and activity clubs.

[3]We consider such cross-subsidies to be DoD expenditures because the installations choose to allocate the "profit" from these other activities to child care when they could use the resources for another purpose.

is also common in employer-provided child care—the employer typically provides the space and contracts with the child-care provider to operate the center.

As a result, our cost estimates should be viewed as being limited to estimating the cost of *operating* DoD child-care programs. These estimates do not include the cost of constructing the facilities used to provide the care. Any policy decision to increase the number of children served in CDCs must take into account such up-front costs. This omission in our cost analysis also leads us to caution readers who are interested in comparing the costs of DoD-run care with other child-care providers' costs: Those costs may include the cost of the space as well as the operating costs. Information from other studies could help an interested reader put our cost estimates into perspective. For example, the GAO (1999) found that the cost of space at Air Force child development centers ranged from 7 to 12 percent of the total costs, depending on the age of the child.

Because of our focus on the cost to consumers, we caution readers that our estimates are not directly comparable with estimates of the per-hour cost per child generated by other studies. Nevertheless, our estimates are relevant to a comparison of the policy options that the DoD faces and to an examination of the cost structure of DoD-operated centers.

INSTALLATION COST SURVEY

Visits to the headquarters of each Service revealed that data at the level of detail needed to determine cost per child by child age were not consistently available at the headquarters level. In order to assess the costs of delivering child care by child age, we had to collect cost data from individual installations.

Sample Selection

We generated a sample of 69 installations with DoD-run child care. In selecting our sample, we had several objectives. First, we wanted to choose enough installations from each Service so that we could generate precise Service-level cost estimates. Second, we wanted to capture variation across installations in terms of the cost of living in each area and the remoteness of each area (that is, its distance from a population center). To be eligible for inclusion in the study sample, an installation had to provide child care on base through at least one CDC. The sample was weighted by the capacity of the CDC so that installations with a large CDC capacity were more likely to be selected into the sample than installations with a small CDC capacity. We selected into our sample 20 Air Force installations, 20 Army installations, 9 Marine Corps installations, and 20 Navy installations.[4] Navy headquarters requested that we send surveys to regional commanders, who would then distribute them to the installations. Surveys were sent to ten commands for distribution.

Our sample selection methodology also considered the cost of living in the installation's local area and its remoteness from the nearest city. We included these variables because we hypothesized that installations in expensive or remote parts of the country might face different (and probably higher) costs than installations in other parts of the country. By considering these attributes of installations in our sampling process, we could control for them in our analyses. To identify high-cost areas, we used the median income of the city in which the installation is located, or, in the case of installations located outside a city, the median income of the city closest to the installation. To identify remote installations, we used a combination of population density information and information on the distance between the installation and the nearest city. Our definition of remoteness was less restrictive than the DoD definition of "isolated and remote."

In addition to generating a sample of installations, we also surveyed all seven DoD sites where center-based care was sponsored by the DoD but provided by a contractor at the time of our survey. These sites included one Air Force base (Vance), one Navy installation (Naval Inventory Control Point [NAVICP] in Mechanicsburg, Pennsylvania), a National Security Agency (NSA) site, and four Defense Logistics Agency (DLA) sites.

---

[4]The sampling frame included 51 Army, 53 Navy, 13 Marine Corps, and 65 Air Force installations. We surveyed a smaller number of Marine Corps installations, but they represent a greater percentage of total Marine Corps installations. This number enabled us to generate cost estimates with a similar level of precision across services.

Survey Sample

Our goal was to create a sample that was representative of military child-care centers in the United States (we did not consider foreign installations) on a number of important dimensions. The sample would allow us to draw inferences about the relationship between cost and specific installation characteristics, such as Military Service and rural versus urban location. To achieve this goal, we created a database that included

- the name and Service affiliation of every DoD installation within the United States that provides center-based child care

- the total CDC capacity on that installation

- an indicator variable ("rich") reflecting whether the installation is in a high cost of living area

- an indicator variable ("remote") reflecting whether the installation is remotely located.

In order to categorize installations as rich or remote, we used a data set assembled by a RAND colleague, Richard Buddin. "Rich" installations are those located in Standard Metropolitan Statistical Areas (SMSAs) in which the median family income is $49,000 per year or higher in current dollars.[5] "Remote" installations are identified by combining information about population density in the SMSA with information on the distance to the nearest city. Based on our preliminary site visits, we hypothesized that installations located in sparsely populated areas and installations that are very far from a population center may be considered remote for our purposes in the sense that it may be difficult to attract civilians to work at the base. We asked former military members familiar with the installations to react to the categorization, and they confirmed that it reflected the type of remoteness that we sought.

---

[5]Information on median income is taken from 1990 census data and reflects 1989 income information on all residents in the local area, not just military personnel. The cut point for the median was $35,000 in 1989 dollars. Approximately 70 percent of DoD installations in our database were located in an area that fell below this cut point, and about 30 percent were above. This characterization of income levels in specified geographic areas does not imply that the income of specific armed services members necessarily achieves the median level.

If the population density of the SMSA is more than 5,000 individuals per square mile, or if the installation is in a city, the installation is *not* considered remote. An installation *is* considered remote if any of the following conditions applies:

- The installation is located in an area with a population density of 2,501 to 5,000 individuals per square mile, *and* it is more than 15 miles from the nearest city.

- The population density is between 1,001 and 2,500 individuals per square mile, *and* the nearest city is more than ten miles away.

- The population density is under 1,000 individuals per square mile, *and* the installation is not located in a city.

Table 3.1 shows the number of installations with CDCs, which served as our sampling frame, for each Service and how they were categorized according to the "rich" and "remote" variables.

As stated earlier, we drew a sample of 69 DoD installations, including 20 from the Air Force, 20 from the Army, 9 from the Marine Corps, and 20 from the Navy. The sample was selected by a random draw from each rich/remote cell (as shown in Table 3.1) for each Service. For each draw, we weighted the installations by the number of CDC slots in their centers so that installations serving larger numbers of children were more likely to be sampled.

Based on the sampling frame shown in Table 3.1, Table 3.2 shows the number of installations we surveyed in each Service and how they were categorized according to the rich and remote variables.

In addition, we surveyed all DoD sites with contractor-provided child care.

In November 1999, we sent our Child Care Cost Survey to the 69 military installations included in our sample; surveys were also sent to six managers of contractor-operated centers. Using a variety of follow-up approaches, we received 65 completed surveys (60 from the DoD installations and 5 from the contract managers) out of the 75 we sent out, for a final completion rate of 88 percent. Table 3.3 presents characteristics of the responding installations.

Table 3.1

Categorization of Installations in the Sampling Frame for the Rich and Remote Variables, by Service

Service	Not Rich and Not Remote	Not Rich and Remote	Rich and Not Remote	Rich and Remote	Total
Army	26	13	8	4	51
Navy	23	8	20	2	53
Air Force	37	16	9	3	65
Marine Corps	4	4	5	0	13
Total	90	41	42	9	182

Table 3.2

Categorization of Installations in the Sample for the Rich and Remote Variables, by Service

Service	Not Rich and Not Remote	Not Rich and Remote	Rich and Not Remote	Rich and Remote	Total
Army	10	4	3	3	20
Navy	8	3	8	1	20
Air Force	10	5	4	1	20
Marine Corps	2	3	4	0	9
Total	30	15	19	5	69

Table 3.3

Categorization of Responding Installations for the Rich and Remote Variables, by Service

Service	Not Rich and Not Remote	Not Rich and Remote	Rich and Not Remote	Rich and Remote	Total
Army	8	4	2	2	16
Navy	8	3	7	1	19
Air Force	10	5	3	0	18
Marine Corps	1	3	3	0	7
Total	27	15	15	3	60

Survey Form

Before drafting the cost survey, we visited three installations repre-senting the Navy, Marine Corps, and Air Force to talk to child-care managers and their supervisors about how cost data are collected and reported. (Efforts to visit an Army installation at that time were not successful.) The goal of these visits was to ensure that the survey would contain questions that installation respondents would be able to answer without too much difficulty and that would allow us to collect comparable data across Services. An additional goal was to minimize the burden on respondents to the greatest extent possible.

In order to assess costs, we developed a 41-item Child Care Cost Survey. The survey includes a series of tables that ask respondents to indicate expenditures and costs by child age and by setting (CDC, FCC, or SAC). Representatives of each of the Services reviewed this form and met with RAND to discuss appropriate changes to the instrument.

To ensure that the survey could be understood and responded to with available data, we sent out surveys to the three installations that we had visited during our preliminary visits. We chose to use these installations because we had some understanding after our visits of how child care was delivered and costs were recorded and managed in those installations. We also met the people who would be completing the form and believed they would be forthcoming about any problems with the form or about the data collection process in general. To facilitate completion of the survey form, we included an optional worksheet to help respondents calculate the personnel costs we asked them to include on the survey form. The survey form can be found in Appendix A.

Cost Analyses

The aim of the cost analyses was to develop estimates of the annual cost to parents and the DoD per child by child age group for FCC and CDC care. Our cost estimates also included estimates for SAC provided in the CDCs.[6] We focused on annual cost because we did not have access to hourly staffing or enrollment information for all Services for CDC care, and no staffing information was available for FCC and contractor-based care.

DoD-Run CDC Cost Estimates

Our survey gathered information on CDC expenditures. In order to develop estimates of the annual[7] cost per child by child age group for DoD-operated CDC care at a particular installation, we designed a procedure for allocating costs to different age groups. First, we divided costs into three types: (1) direct-care labor costs, (2) food costs, and (3) other costs. Direct-care labor costs include the cost of wages and benefits for primary caregivers (both NAF and APF staff) and their assistants.[8] These are individuals who are working in the centers directly in a caregiving capacity. Food costs include any costs associated with purchasing, preparing, or delivering food, as well as the costs associated with managing a food program. Other costs include all labor costs not considered direct-care labor[9] (such as training and curriculum specialists, center management, program management, receptionists, custodial services, and administration), as well as operational expenses, such as utilities, minor construction, maintenance, repair, and postage and supplies.

---

[6]SAC is treated differently on different installations and in different services. Some SAC is considered part of the CDP and is provided in CDCs. This care is included in our analysis. Most SAC, however, is provided in youth centers or at elementary schools (for example, in before- and after-school programs). Often, these programs are operated through a completely separate program under a different budget. Because of the variety of mechanisms through which SAC is provided, a comprehensive analysis of SAC was beyond the scope of our effort.

[7]For the Army, Navy, and Air Force, annual costs are for fiscal year 1998, which runs from October 1997 to September 1998. For Marine Corps installations, NAF annual costs are reported for business year 1998, which runs from January 1998 to December 1998 and APF annual costs are for fiscal year 1998, which runs from October 1997 to September 1998.

[8]As we describe later, our cost-allocation methodology treats all caregiver labor costs as "direct care" costs. Thus, any paid time that caregivers spend outside the classroom (for example, for breaks or for training) is treated as a direct labor cost.

[9]Our survey requested information on the percentage of time that program administrators devoted to various CDP activities (CDC, FCC, or SAC); the personnel costs were allocated accordingly to those programs.

Although the survey did include a line item for rent, DoD-run centers generally do not pay rent for facilities. In the few instances in which installations reported a rental expense, it was for equipment rental (for example, a photocopy machine). Direct-care labor costs were totaled and then allocated to children enrolled as of March 1998 in different age groups according to the minimum caregiver-to-child ratios required by the DoD. We determined through our preliminary interviews that it would not be possible to gather reliable staffing information linking the exact number and grade level of caregivers to child age groups. As a result, we adopted the following approach for allocating direct-care costs to children by age group (see Chapter Four for a definition of the age groups).

First, we calculated the hypothetical number of adults[10] required for care of enrolled children by age group. We divided the number of enrolled children by the minimum DoD adult-to-child ratio for that age group (1-to-4 for infants, 1-to-5 for pre-toddlers, 1-to-7 for toddlers, 1-to-12 for preschool, and 1-to-15 for school-age). We then took the total direct-care personnel costs and divided those costs by the number of hypothetical adults required to staff the center to get an average cost per hypothetical caregiver. The cost per caregiver was then divided by the minimum ratio for the age group in order to generate an estimate of the cost per child in that age group.

The procedure we describe incorporates two important assumptions. First, it assumes that any over- or understaffing relative to the minimum DoD ratios is spread equally, in percentage terms, across the age groups. In other words, if an installation is "overstaffed" by 10 percent relative to the DoD ratios, then we are assuming that the infant room is overstaffed by 10 percent, the pre-toddler room is overstaffed by 10 percent, and so on.[11] The approach also assumes

---

[10]By "hypothetical number of adults," we mean the number of adults who would be required to staff the center at any given time if it were operating exactly in accordance with the minimum DoD ratios with no understaffing or overstaffing.

[11]Although this assumption is not likely to hold on any given day, our preliminary site visits to DoD centers suggested that over the course of an entire year, over- or understaffing (due to turnover, illness, and such) would be spread across the age groups in proportion to the number of total caregivers serving that age group. Our preliminary site visits revealed a tendency for child development centers to be "overstaffed" relative to minimum DoD ratios to allow for floaters who would cover for

that the average cost of a caregiver is the same for all age groups; in other words, infant caregivers are paid (on average) the same amount as preschool caregivers.[12] This assumption is consistent with policies that base pay on skills, experience, and training, and not on the age of children served.

Food costs were allocated on a per-child basis to all children except infants.[13] Other costs were allocated equally on a per-child basis to all children: Any food purchases that might appropriately be allocated to or shared by infants (for example, purchase of formula with APF expenditures) were captured in other costs.

The estimate of the annual cost per child in a particular age group at an installation is the sum of three components:

1. the estimated annual direct-care labor costs per child for that age group at that installation

2. the estimated food cost per child at that installation

3. other estimated costs per child at that installation, including costs for utilities, supplies, custodial services, training and curriculum specialists, center administration, program administration and management, background checks, and other items.

FCC Costs

In some respects, it is more challenging to construct cost estimates per child for FCC. Whereas with the CDC estimates we were able to focus on expenditures and allocate those expenditures across age groups, with FCC, the providers work essentially as independent contractors. As a result, we have no way of capturing their expendi-

---

the primary caregivers during breaks, illness, or training. We did not observe any instances of classroom staffing levels that exceeded DoD minimum ratios.

[12]Information on the grade and salary level of caregivers assigned to specific age groups is not consistently available. However, the detailed staffing information we collected during our preliminary site visits revealed no systematic staffing patterns, such as more highly graded (and highly paid) caregivers staffing infant or preschool rooms.

[13]The food cost component is not included for infants because providing food to infants is not a consistent practice across the programs analyzed. Some programs rely on parents to supply food for their infants.

tures. A study of the fees paid by parents to FCC providers and their expenditures would provide very useful information to the DoD.

In the absence of good expenditure data, we gathered information on the average weekly parent fee paid to FCC providers by age group, the other costs of running the FCC program, and the U.S. Department of Agriculture (USDA) food program payments made to FCC providers. The estimate of the annual FCC cost per child in a particular age group at a given installation consisted of three components:

1. the estimated weekly fee plus the DoD subsidy paid to providers, multiplied by 52

2. the estimated FCC food cost per child at that installation

3. the estimated FCC "other costs per child" at that installation.

The estimated food cost per child was calculated as the total FCC USDA payments divided by the number of children (excluding infants) served[14] in FCC. The estimated "other costs" were calculated as the total program administration costs, which include personnel and supplies. Other costs for FCC include inspection, training for providers, communal supplies such as the lending library, and general administration. "Other costs per child" are the total other costs divided by the number of children served in FCC.

Contractor CDC Cost Estimates

As with the FCC cost estimates, we did not have access to information on actual expenditures for contractor-provided care. Instead, our estimates were based on DoD payments to the contractors, costs incurred by the DoD in administering the contract, plus information on parent fees paid to the contractors. As with FCC, it is important to note that parent fees are not the same as provider expenditures. An important consideration in calculating contractor costs is that in some community-based child-care centers, fees charged for infants capture less than the full cost of care, whereas fees for older children exceed costs and permit some cross-subsidy to infants. (This is done to reduce what would otherwise be extremely high fees for infant

---

[14]The total number of children served in FCC includes both the children of the FCC providers under the age of eight, as well as other children cared for by the providers.

care.) Because our contractor cost estimates are based on these fees, it is important to understand that our estimates of cost per child by age group for contractor-provided care should be viewed as being extremely rough. Nonetheless, they provide a useful point of comparison with the estimates for DoD-run CDC care.

The contractor CDC estimates consist of two components: one that is related to the age of the child and one that is not. *Age-related costs* are payments to the contractor that vary depending on the age of the children served. These typically take the form of weekly fees to the contractor, based on enrollment. These fees may be borne entirely by parents, or by parents and the DoD. *Non–age-related costs* include payments to contractors (for example, additional payments for center operation, for the mortgage on the building, or for equipment), plus the costs (mainly personnel) associated with monitoring and administering the contract. These costs are totaled and then allocated on a per-child basis to all children served through the DoD contract. These costs are typically incurred by the DoD and not by parents.

CIVILIAN CENTER VISITS

We sought out a small number of civilian child-care centers that we could visit to help us better contextualize and understand the costs and trade-offs being made by the military centers in our sample. The sponsoring employers subsidized all of the civilian centers we selected at a high rate. Like the military CDCs that are at the core of our study, each civilian center is located at the employment site.

We selected four of the seven civilian centers we visited from a list of family-friendly employers—the "100 Best Companies for Families"—published each year by *Working Mother* magazine. Entries on that list are not selected at random. Typically, someone in a company's HR department determines that it is in the company's interest to appear on the list. An application must be filled out and supporting materials sent to the magazine. Six criteria are applied in determining whether a company will make the list: pay; opportunities for women to advance; child care; flexibility in work hours and work assignments; work/life resources, such as counseling; support groups; and other family-friendly benefits, such as extended parental leave and adoption and elder care.

Companies that appear on the *Working Mother* list are proud of their efforts to provide a family-friendly environment, including, in more than half of the cases, on-site child care for their employees' children. Sixty-one percent of the centers that are listed on the 100-best-companies list are accredited—a very high percentage for the civilian sector, in which overall accreditation rates are under 10 percent (Campbell et al., 2000). Everyone we interviewed at the civilian child-care centers we selected from the *Working Mother* list viewed the effort to get on, and stay on, the list as a recruiting tool and a signal of corporate caring that also improves employee morale and retention.

We lacked the necessary resources to interview a representative sample of centers. Instead, we focused on employers that appeared roughly similar to military centers with regard to two key factors: level of subsidization of the center and accreditation status. We selected employers who subsidized their centers at rates roughly comparable to those of the military (50 to 70 percent) and that provided an accredited center, given that the military requires its centers to be accredited.

We also visited two on-site centers subsidized by the GSA, which is considered to be the federal government's "landlord" because it manages federal property. A final center that we visited provides care to the children of employees of the Pentagon.[15] All of the centers of which we requested a visit agreed to host us. In all instances, we chose centers that we could access fairly easily; for the GSA centers, this was the major criterion for selection.

At each center we visited, we took a brief tour and met with the center's director. Using a semistructured interview form, we queried each director on many of the same issues that we had explored in our cost survey of the military installations—for example, child-to-adult ratios, parent fees, and level of subsidy. These interviews averaged more than an hour in length. Whenever possible, we also conducted an interview with the staff member in the sponsoring company's HR department who was responsible for overseeing or providing liaison with the child-care center. In a few cases, these were joint interviews with the oversight person and the child-care center director, but in

---

[15]The Pentagon center is not a military CDC because the Pentagon is not a military installation.

most cases the oversight person and the director were interviewed separately. We interviewed a total of five HR people in three centers.

Of the seven centers we visited, four of the non-GSA centers and one of the two GSA centers were operated by an outside contractor. We were able to interview representatives for two contractors who operated three of the centers that we visited. Interviews with the contractors focused on relationships with employers, how to work with subsidies of various sizes, and how a contractor translates an employer's vision and goals into a working child-care center. We also conducted two interviews with GSA personnel, one at the local level (in Los Angeles) and one at the regional level (in San Francisco). Issues similar to those addressed by the contractors were discussed with GSA staff.

Interview notes were written up soon after each of our interviews with civilian child-care center staff using the semistructured interview guide to structure the notes. Our analyses focused on key attributes of the centers; employer policies with regard to quality, fees, and subsidies; and the effects of these policies on access to each center, enrollment, operations, and program quality. Comparisons were made across care centers based on key employer attributes, such as company size and subsidy policies.

Chapter Four

COSTS OF CDC, FCC, AND CONTRACTOR-
PROVIDED CARE

In this chapter, we first present our analyses of basic CDC cost data. Then, we go on to examine some of the cross-Service and cross-installation variations in CDC operations and CDC organization that help to explain these differences. We then present per-child costs for FCC care. As was done with the CDC data, we examine some of the cross-Service and cross-installation variations that might help to explain FCC cost differences. We also examine the contribution of subsidies to FCC. We conclude with a discussion of costs in contractor-operated centers.

Our analyses assume that care provided in all settings and in all Services is of comparable quality. We are forced to make this assumption because we could not assess quality within the scope of the study. The fact that all centers included in the study are accredited makes this assumption more tenable, although it is certainly true that quality can vary considerably across accredited centers.

COSTS FOR CDC CARE

Average annual cost per child in CDC care is closely linked to a child's age, as shown in Table 4.1. This result is driven by what we know about the delivery of child care—with fewer children per caregiver permitted at younger ages, it simply costs more to care for younger children than older children. Comparing average annual cost for infants with that for preschoolers, it is apparent that costs for the former group are almost double what they are for the latter

Table 4.1

Average Annual Cost Per Child and Maximum Caregiver-to-Child Ratios in CDC Care, by Child Age

Child Age	Maximum Allowable Caregiver-to-Child Ratios[a]	Average Annual Cost
Infant (6 weeks–12 months)	1:4	$12,133
Pre-toddler (12–23 months)	1:5	$10,825
Toddler (24–35 months)	1:7	$8,743
Preschool (36 months–5 years)	1:12	$6,594
School-age (kindergarten and up)[b]	1:15	$4,595

[a]Ratios are specified in Department of Defense Instruction (DoDI) 6060.2, January 19, 1993.

[b]These programs involve fewer hours of care per child, although part-day public school kindergarten programs that often last just two hours reduce the hours per child for the youngest children in this age category only slightly.

group. These huge cost differences are not surprising when one examines the Maximum Allowable Ratios column: the caregiver-to-child ratio is three times larger for preschoolers than it is for infants.

For the reasons we just described, we were not able to calculate costs on an hourly basis. However, we can use reasonable assumptions to generate a rough way of translating hourly costs into annual costs. For example, if we assume that full-time center enrollment involves 2,500 hours per year of care (10 hours a day, 5 days a week, for 50 weeks a year), we find that the cost figures that we produced from our survey are lower than those found by the GAO in its study of child-care costs in Air Force Centers (GAO, 1999). Using this multiplier, the GAO hourly cost estimates would translate into $13,575 for infants; $11,800 for pre-toddlers; $9,900 for toddlers; and $8,075 for preschoolers.

Part of the difference between our estimates and the GAO estimates is accounted for by the fact that the GAO cost figures included estimates of the rental cost of space, the value of donated time, and the value of legal services, all of which were not included in our analysis. As emphasized by the GAO study, these costs are higher than those reported by the Colorado Cost, Quality, and Child Outcomes in Child Care Centers Study (Cost, Quality, and Child Outcomes Study Team,

1995). But the reasons for these differences are understandable. The cost figures from the Colorado study are based on centers that were providing, on average, mediocre care. The Colorado study concluded that high-quality care is more costly to provide; the increment in cost to provide high-quality care depends on the preexisting quality level. Further, the Colorado study's cost estimates are based on data collected in 1993.

Table 4.2 presents average annual cost data by Service. Only a limited number of installations reported that they provided SAC in CDCs; we estimated SAC costs if the care was provided outside the CDC, as long as the care was funded with child development resources. Consequently, none of the cross-Service comparisons on SAC costs are statistically significant and we focus our discussion on younger children. As shown in Table 4.2, the annual cost per child in CDC care is highest in the Navy. Moreover, this ranking holds true for each child-age category.[1] The Marine Corps ranks lowest in per-child average cost.[2]

Table 4.3 reports our estimates of food costs and other costs (as described in Chapter Three). Other costs are higher in the Navy than in the other Services. These differences are statistically significant at the 5-percent level. Comparison of the Navy's other costs with those of the other Services reveals that the Navy's other costs are more than $1,000 per child over those of the next-highest Service, the Air Force. However, the cost differential at each child age level (see Table 4.2) between the Navy's average cost and that of the Air Force, the next-highest Service, exceeds this difference. The Army's food cost per child is higher than in the Marine Corps (statistically significant at the 5-percent level), but other cross-Service differences in food costs are not significant.

---

[1]Differences between the Navy and Air Force for infant and pre-toddler care costs are significant at the 10-percent level. All other differences are significant at the 5-percent level.

[2]The differences between the Marine Corps and the Navy, and between the Marine Corps and the Air Force, are significant at all age levels at the 5-percent level. The differences between Army and Marine Corps costs are not significant.

Table 4.2

Average Annual Cost Per Child in CDC Care, by Child Age and Service

Child Age	Army	Navy	Air Force	Marine Corps
Infant (6 weeks–12 months)	$10,482	$14,438	$12,177	$9,874
Pre-toddler (12–23 months)	$9,425	$12,900	$10,807	$8,737
Toddler (24–35 months)	$7,544	$10,596	$8,641	$6,982
Preschool (36 months– 5 years)	$5,585	$8,197	$6,449	$5,154
School-age (kindergarten and up) [a]	$4,710	—	$4,167	$4,530

[a]Numbers of CDCs with school-age care programs were low: Only 11 installations provided such care (six in the Army, one in the Air Force, and four in the Marine Corps). Consequently, cross-Service comparisons for this age group should be regarded as tentative.

Table 4.3

Average Other Costs and Food Costs Per Child in CDC Care, by Service

	All Services	Army	Navy	Air Force	Marine Corps
CDC other costs	$3,084	$2,255	$4,358	$2,893	$2,194
CDC food costs[a]	$502	$587	$479	$488	$399

[a]Not attributable to infants.

Possible explanations for Service differences in per-child CDC costs might be traced to cross-Service differences in the number of children served, the age distribution of children served, or average CDC size.[3] It has been established that with a range of fixed costs (for example, the director's salary), larger centers can care for children at a lower per-child cost. Indeed, the military has identified CDC sizes below which costs per child become unacceptably high (Smith, 2000).

---

[3]Installations often operate more than one CDC. The average size of CDCs on an installation is simply the total number of children served divided by the number of CDCs at that installation. The total number of children served in CDCs on an installation differs from the average CDC size on an installation if the installation has more than one CDC.

As shown in Table 4.4, the number of children served at an installation varies considerably by Service. In particular, Army installations provide care to more children in every age group.[4] Navy installations, which we found to have the highest per-child costs, tend to serve the fewest children.

Despite the aforementioned difference in the number of children served, the distribution of children served across age groups appears to be similar across all Services, as reflected in Table 4.5. For example, the overall percentage of preschoolers, across Services, is 50 percent. The Army's percentage, 48 percent, is slightly *below* this cross-Service average, although it is slightly higher than the Navy's 45 percent.

Although it is useful to consider the total number of children served by CDCs on an installation, the average size of CDCs might also have an important impact on costs. An installation that serves 500 children in ten centers might be less efficient than an installation that

Table 4.4

Average Number of Children in CDC Care at an Installation, by Child Age and Service

Child Age	All Services	Army	Navy	Air Force	Marine Corps
Infant (6 weeks–12 months)	27.7	47.7	20.4	21.7	17.6
Pre-toddler (12–23 months)	39.0	61.2	29.3	31.7	33.1
Toddler (24–35 months)	55.2	81.6	42.1	47.4	50.0
Preschool (36 months–5 years)	126.0	186.9	80.5	127.3	100.5
School-age (kindergarten and up)[a]	22.1	19	—	12.0	29.4
Total[b]	251.2	384.5	172.2	228.8	217.9

[a]These numbers apply only to the 11 installations that provide school-age care.

[b]Totals include school-age care, if it is provided.

_____

[4]The difference between the number of children served by Army installations and other installations is statistically significant at the 5-percent level for all age groups.

serves 500 children in two centers. Table 4.6 reports the average size (number of children served) of CDCs by Service. With an average size of 127.9, Navy centers are, on average, the smallest in the DoD. This size difference is significant at the 5-percent level for the Army and Air Force and at the 10-percent level for the Marine Corps. The average size of Army centers is 204.5, which makes them larger than both Navy centers (significant at the 5-percent level) and Air Force centers (significant at the 10-percent level).

To better understand the factors that influence CDC costs, we developed regression models for the costs for each child-age group. These regressions enable us to control for characteristics of the installation, the average size of CDCs, the affluence of the area in which the installation is located, the percentage of all children served who are infants and toddlers, and military Service. We selected these factors because it seemed plausible that each might bear on the amount of money being spent per child for care.

Table 4.5

Percentage of Children in Each Age Group in CDC Care, by Service

Child Age	All Services	Army	Navy	Air Force	Marine Corps
Infant (6 weeks–12 months)	11%	12%	12%	9%	11%
Pre-toddler (12–23 months)	15%	14%	18%	14%	15%
Toddler (24–35 months)	22%	21%	25%	20%	24%
Preschool (36 months–5 years)	50%	48%	45%	56%	45%

NOTE: Percentages do not sum to 100 because we have not included school-age care.

Table 4.6

Average Center Size, by Service

	All Services	Army	Navy	Air Force	Marine Corps
Center size (number of children served)	165.8	204.5	127.9	168.3	173.3

Remoteness seemed to be a plausible contributor because, in more-isolated areas, parents would have fewer child-care choices and CDCs might feel less of a need to compete with community-based providers for the enrollment of military children. In addition, military spouses, who constitute the majority of caregivers, may have few other alternatives to CDC jobs. At the same time, it may be more difficult to attract caregivers who are not military spouses. In one of our pretest sites, which was isolated but not technically remote, we were told that it is difficult to find and keep CDC caregivers.

Average size of CDCs on the installation was, we believed, likely to affect costs because many CDC costs are fixed. With more children in care, these costs are spread over a greater number of children, thereby reducing these costs at the per-child level.

In terms of *affluence*, it seemed plausible on its face that installations located in more-affluent areas might put more resources behind each child in care. These higher costs would be more acceptable to CDC patrons accustomed to relatively high community-care costs. Moreover, in more-affluent areas, it might prove necessary to pay higher caregiver wages and to spend more for supplies and services.[5] Finally, because one of our research questions was whether there are differences across the Services in child-care costs, we included military Service in our model.

We summarize the regression results here; a more detailed discussion is available in Appendix B. The results of our regressions reveal that in every age group, child-care costs are positively associated with cost of living in the area: They are significantly higher in areas with a higher cost of living.[6] Whether these findings reflect higher labor costs in these areas, or the feeling that parents will more easily

---

[5]Indeed, the federal government has instituted a locality pay system under which many federal civil service employees who work in high-cost-of-living areas receive a higher wage. The locality pay differential is based on the location of employment and not on residence. In FY 1998, there were 32 locality pay regions with locality pay percentages ranging from 5.42 percent (for the "Rest of U.S." category) to 12.06 percent (for the San Francisco-Oakland-San Jose region). For FY 2000, the range was 6.78 percent to 16.98 percent. The terminology is slightly confusing because everybody gets some locality pay because one "region" encompasses the "Rest of the U.S."

[6]We define *cost of living* with reference to the median income in the local area in which the installation is located.

tolerate being on the higher end of the DoD fee range, or some combination of these two factors or other factors, cannot be determined from our data.

The regressions also reveal that average center size is significantly related to per-child CDC costs for all age groups, with larger centers associated with lower costs. This result is consistent with the hypothesis that larger centers are able to implement more-efficient staffing procedures than smaller centers. For example, a large center and a small center might each have one floater to cover for sick caregivers or caregivers on break. The cost of this floater is spread across a greater number of "required adult caregivers" in a large center, so the cost per adult caregiver is larger by comparison in the small center. This difference in cost per required caregiver has more impact on the cost per infant than on the cost per preschool-age child because of the higher staff-to-child ratios required for younger children.

Finally, we found that per-child CDC costs were higher in the Navy and the Air Force than in the Marine Corps, even after controlling for other factors.[7] These findings mirror those shown in Table 4.2 but make clear that these effects are not a function of differences across Services in installation affluence or remoteness, or of the number of children in CDC care.[8]

We also estimated separate regression equations for the three CDC care cost components: other costs per child, food costs per child, and direct-labor costs per child. These regressions revealed that installations with more children per center have lower other costs *and* lower direct-care labor costs. The magnitude of the impact of average center size on the two cost components is approximately the same. This suggests that larger centers are able to reduce the cost per child through economies of scale in indirect or administrative costs and

---

[7]There was no statistically significant difference between the Army estimates and those of the other services.

[8]One reviewer of the draft document of this report noted that higher costs in the Navy are likely due to the Navy's tendency to use greater numbers of APF staff than the other services. While we could not test this hypothesis directly with our data, our analysis of total APF and NAF expenditures on CDP activities, presented later in this chapter, supports this notion. NAF expenditures account for 35 percent of total expenditures in the Navy and about 50 percent of the total in the other services.

through a more efficient use of direct-care staff.[9] Service-level variables were not significant in these regression analyses of other costs, suggesting that differences in the average indirect cost by Service, reported earlier in Table 4.3, are driven by other factors, such as average center size.

The cost of living in the local area appears to impact only direct-care labor costs.[10] This is not surprising in view of the fact that federal government wages are tied to a locale's cost of living through locality pay.

Our regressions also suggest that the Service differences reported earlier in this chapter are primarily driven by differences in direct-care labor costs. Direct-care labor costs per child are higher in the Navy and the Air Force than in the Marine Corps.[11]

COSTS FOR FCC

In much the same way that we computed per-child costs for CDC care, we computed per-child costs for FCC. As shown in Table 4.7, the average annual cost per child in FCC is considerably lower than the average per-child cost of care in CDCs.

As shown in Table 4.8, per-child costs in FCC do not vary dramatically by Service or by age. Indeed, there is no statistically significant cross-Service variation in costs, and with the exception of school-age care, there is no significant variation by age. This contrasts markedly with the age and Service variation evident in CDC costs. This is due to the fact that the child-staff ratios in CDC care and FCC differ; in CDCs they increase gradually with age, whereas in FCC the key distinctions are between infants, pre-toddlers, and older children, with a cap of six children total in each FCC home. What is also noteworthy about Table 4.8 is the low "other costs," which is not surprising given that administration is necessarily off-site (although on base) and

---

[9]These relationships are statistically significant at the 1-percent level.

[10]The parameter estimate for direct-care infant labor costs on income was positive and significant at the 5-percent level.

[11]For infants, the parameter estimates on the Air Force are positive and significant at the 5-percent level, and the estimates on the Navy are positive and significant at the 10-percent (but not at the 5-percent) level.

Table 4.7

Average Annual Cost Per Child in FCC, by Child Age

Child Age	Maximum Allowable Number of Children[a]	Average Annual Cost[b]
Infant (6 weeks–12 months)	Two, when there are also older children in the FCC household; three, when only infants are cared for in the FCC household	$5,014
Pre-toddler (12–23 months)	Two, when there are also older children; three, when only pre-toddlers are cared for	$5,118
Toddler (24–35 months)	Total number of children who can be cared for in an FCC household is six	$4,609
Preschool (36 months–5 years)	Total number of children who can be cared for in an FCC household is six	$4,512
School-age (kindergarten and up)[c]	Six, when there are also younger children; eight, when only school-age children are cared for (including the provider's own children)	$3,293

[a]In every instance, the provider's own children under the age of eight must be counted in these figures.

[b]The entries in this column represent total cost, which includes cost to both families and the Service.

[c]These programs involve fewer hours of care per child, although part-day public school kindergarten programs that often last just two hours reduce the hours per child for the youngest children in this age category only slightly.

part-time.[12] Administrators usually consist of one or more FCC coordinators, depending on the number of homes. Coordinators are responsible for multiple FCC homes, so that the cost of their salaries is spread across multiple homes and multiple children.

A direct comparison of CDCs and FCC food costs is not appropriate because we could measure only USDA payments to providers, which don't capture the full cost of providing food to children.

---

[12]FCC administrators generally visit homes several times a month. Although CDC administrators spend only limited time in each classroom, they are on-site full time.

Table 4.8

Average Annual Cost Per Child in FCC, by Service[a]

Child Age	All Services	Army	Navy	Air Force	Marine Corps
Infant (6 weeks–12 months)	$5,014	$4,713	$5,081	$4,922	$5,763
Pre-toddler (12–23 months)	$5,118	$4,858	$5,340	$4,864	$5,883
Toddler (24–35 months)	$4,609	$4,782	$4,307	$4,773	$4,450
Preschool (36 months–5 years)	$4,512	$4,657	$4,411	$4,523	$4,361
School-age (kindergarten and up)	$3,293	$3,576	$3,121	$3,341	$2,830
Average FCC other costs	$317	$401	$267	$285	$318
Average FCC food costs	$334	$432	$367	$249	$272

[a]Age categories are specified in DoDI 6060.2, January 19, 1993.

Table 4.9 presents the median percentages of children in each age group in FCC by Service. What is apparent from this table is that the age distribution in FCC homes is flatter than it is in the CDCs. The difference in percentages between the best-represented and least-represented age group is never more than 16 percent. Comparable figures for the CDC age distributions begin at 34 percent and go as high as 47 percent. Two factors appear to account for this effect. First, there are relatively more infants in FCC, although the CDC-FCC differences in this category are not large. More significantly, the percentage of preschoolers in CDCs is substantially higher than in FCC homes. This reflects the larger number of slots available in CDCs for preschool care.

As we had done with the CDC costs, we conducted regression analyses on FCC cost estimates by age group to identify any relationships between FCC costs and service, FCC costs and the cost of living in the local area, or FCC costs and remoteness. We found that income was significantly related (at the 5-percent level) to FCC costs for all age groups and to FCC other costs for all age groups. Installations located in areas with higher costs of living had higher FCC costs. Parameter

Table 4.9

Median Percentage of Children in Each Age Group in FCC, by Service

Child Age	All Services	Army	Navy	Air Force	Marine Corps
Infant (6 weeks–12 months)	14%	16%	14%	14%	13%
Pre-toddler (12–23 months)	16%	13%	20%	14%	17%
Toddler (24–35 months)	19%	19%	19%	19%	18%
Preschool (36 months–5 years)	28%	25%	29%	30%	17%
School-age (kindergarten and up)	20%	22%	20%	20%	26%

estimates on Service variables or remoteness were not significantly different from zero.

Some, but by no means all, installations offer a subsidy for FCC care in the form of a direct payment from the DoD to the FCC provider. This payment is in addition to fees paid directly by parents to the provider. As noted in Chapter Two, subsidies have been made available to FCC providers to meet a variety of policy goals, including increasing the total number of available slots, increasing the number of infant slots, and making FCC more affordable by bringing fees in line with those of the CDC. We found that, in general, FCC subsidies for age-specific care during normal hours are not in widespread use.[13] Only 14 of the 60 installations responding to our survey indicated that they provided such a subsidy to FCC providers in fiscal year (FY) 1998. As shown in Table 4.10, most of these subsidies are targeted to infant care; only a few installations provide subsidies for preschoolers or SAC.[14]

---

[13]Included in these calculations are subsidies that apply to all children. The amount of this subsidy was applied to each age group. We are excluding here subsidies for children with special needs, subsidies for after-hours care, or subsidies for greater affordability.

[14]Installations that provide FCC subsidies for preschoolers also subsidize care for younger children.

Table 4.10

Provision of FCC Subsidies: Number of Subsidies by Child Age and Service

Child Age	All Services	Army[a]	Navy	Air Force[b]	Marine Corps
Infant (6 weeks–12 months)	14[c]	6	5	0	3
Pre-toddler (12–23 months)	8	0	5	0	3
Toddler (24–35 months)	8	0	5	0	3
Preschool (36 months–5 years)	3	0	2	0	1
School-age (kindergarten and up)	3	2	0	0	1

[a]This table focuses on subsidies for age-specific care. The Army does not provide such age-specific care subsidies to pre-toddlers, toddlers, and preschoolers.

[b]At the time of our survey, the Air Force had decided not to provide FCC subsidies as a matter of policy.

[c]This entry refers to the number of installations providing the subsidy.

As part of its Child Development System Expansion and Marketing Plan, the DoD came up with a number of initiatives—both subsidies and nonmonetary incentives—designed to increase in-home care availability and services. Notable are the Army's Child Development Group homes and fee equity for families with Category I incomes (see Table 2.1); the Navy's Child Development Home marketing study and provider and caregiver recruitment campaigns; the Marine Corps' pilot effort to provide off-base FCC using nonmilitary providers; and the Air Force's Extended Duty Child Care Program for higher housing priority and larger-housing-unit eligibility for providers. For all Services, this DoD plan suggests more use of FCC subsidies to meet multiple needs.

The size of the FCC subsidy also varied with child age, as shown in Table 4.11. Subsidies for pre-toddlers and toddlers were the highest, with the median subsidy for these groups close to $40 a week. The higher subsidy levels for these age groups are somewhat counter-intuitive: One might expect infant subsidies to be highest because FCC regulations limit the number of infants and pre-toddlers under an FCC caregiver's care; if the caregiver accepts three infants or three pre-toddlers, she may not care for any other children. The reason for

Table 4.11

Median FCC Subsidy Per Week, by Child Age, at Installations Providing a Subsidy

Child Age	Minimum FCC Subsidy	Median FCC Subsidy	Maximum FCC Subsidy
Infant (6 weeks–12 months)	$6	$21.50	$90
Pre-toddler (12–23 months)	$3	$37.50	$90
Toddler (24–35 months)	$14	$38.50	$90
Preschool (36 months– 5 years)	$10	$12.00	$18
School-age (kindergarten and up)	$1	$15	$18

NOTE: The maximum number of installations providing these subsidies was 14.

this pattern of higher non-infant subsidies is that most installations that provide any subsidy provide only an infant subsidy. Those installations that also provide subsidies to older age groups tend to provide relatively high subsidies for all the age groups that they subsidize. In contrast, installations that provide only an infant subsidy tend to subsidize at a low rate. Consequently, the median infant subsidy, which includes both high- and low-subsidy-rate installations, is lower than the median rate for the older age groups, which do not include any low-subsidy installations.

Another unique aspect of FCC is that, for many providers, delivering child care in their own quarters provides a way to earn money while continuing to be able to care for their own young children.[15] How to think about these children in the context of a study of child-care cost is a matter of some discussion; they are not "paying customers," but they do occupy FCC slots. Moreover, if their mothers or fathers were not providing FCC, some portion of those children would be seeking and filling CDC or FCC slots.

In discussions with our study sponsor, we agreed that these children would be considered "full patrons" for purposes of coming up with cost estimates. In other words, they are included in the total number

---

[15] If these providers chose to work in a CDC, they would almost certainly not be caring for their own children there. It is generally agreed that caregivers should not care for their own children in CDCs, as they might be inclined to favor them, although exceptions to this rule do occur in some parent cooperatives.

of children served through FCC. From a cost-estimation perspective, this means that the indirect costs of operating the FCC program are spread across a larger number of children, and thus the other costs per child are lower than they would be otherwise. At the same time, we thought it was important to understand their prevalence in our sample. As shown in Table 4.12, the percentage of the providers' own children served in FCC is nontrivial, with the median across Services at 28 percent. As the table shows, these percentages vary only slightly across Services.

APF AND NAF EXPENDITURES

As we have discussed in this report, military child care is an example of employer-sponsored child care. The costs of providing care are shared by both the DoD and parents. A natural question that arises then is, What fraction of the cost is borne by the DoD and what fraction is borne by the parents?

In light of the cost estimates presented in this chapter, it is evident that the answer will depend on a variety of factors including Service and child age. We did not have access to data on parent fees, however, and therefore we cannot answer the cost-sharing question directly. Nevertheless, we can examine two issues that are related to that question.

First, we can examine the average cost per child for DoD CDC care for children of different age groups and compare it to the average annual parent payment. As discussed in Chapter Two, in FY 1998, average DoD weekly parent fees for military child care ranged from $49 to $93, depending on the parents' total family income. In each Service, the median parent paid the Category III fee, as shown in Table 2.1 of Chapter Two. Using the DoD average Category III fee, and assuming that parents pay for 50 weeks of care per year, we construct a

Table 4.12

Median Percentage of a Provider's Own Children Served in FCC, by Service

All Services	Army	Navy	Air Force	Marine Corps
28%	29%	31%	28%	22%

"typical" parent fee of $3,500 per year.[16] If we divide the typical parent fee by our annual cost estimates, we find that the percentage of total cost covered by the parent fees increases as children move into older age groups (see Table 4.13). The largest subsidy is provided to parents of infants and the smallest subsidy is provided to parents of children in school-age care.

Our analyses revealed that total costs for CDC care varied by Service and that the Services have slightly different average fees at the same income level. Not surprisingly then, the percentage of total costs covered by parent fees also varies by Service. For example, the Category III fee covers 36 percent of the cost of infant care in the Marine Corps but only 25 percent of the cost of infant care in the Navy.

Another way to examine the percentage of child-development program costs covered by the DoD versus those covered by parent fees is to compare APF expenditures with NAF expenditures. As discussed in Chapter Three, NAF expenditures are derived from parent fees or from revenue generated through other NAF activities on an installation, such as from activities clubs or golf course fees. APF expenditures are DoD expenditures. Table 4.14 reports NAF expenditures as

Table 4.13

Percentage of Average Costs Covered by the Category III Parent Fee, by Child Age

Child Age	Average Annual Cost	Parent Fee as a Percent of Cost
Infant (6 weeks–12 months)	$12,133	29%
Pre-toddler (12–23 months)	$10,825	32%
Toddler (24–35 months)	$8,743	40%
Preschool (36 months–5 years)	$6,594	53%
School-age (kindergarten and up)	$4,595	76%

---

[16]The annual fee would be $2,450 for Category I and $4,650 for Category V. Some CDCs charge for 52 weeks per year. Using this figure would change estimates only slightly (for example, a less than 1-percent increase paid by parent). The percentages we report in Table 4.13 vary with the income category of the parent. High-income parents receive a lower subsidy than low-income parents do.

Table 4.14

NAF Expenditures as a Percentage of Total Child-Development Program Expenditures

All Services	Army	Navy	Air Force	Marine Corps
44%	50%	34%	48%	49%

a percentage of total child-development program expenditures for the DoD and for each Service. This analysis reveals that NAF funds cover a lower percentage of CDP expenditures in the Navy than in the other Services.[17]

COST OF CONTRACTOR-PROVIDED CARE

As discussed in the Summary of this report, the DoD recently has focused on streamlining and outsourcing support activities, such as child care. To learn more about the costs of this approach, we surveyed DoD installations and agency locations that provide contractor-operated child care to employees. However, there are relatively few examples of contractor-based DoD CDCs. We received responses from five sites.

As part of this research project, the survey asked for enrollment and cost information, as well as information on nonmonetary support provided by the DoD to the contractor. As discussed in Chapter Three, the cost information we collected captures the costs incurred by both the DoD and parents.

It is worth noting that the contractor-based sites differ from the larger sample of DoD-operated CDCs in several respects. First, most are run by DoD agencies and cater mainly to civilian, rather than military, personnel. Second, in one of the centers, parent fees need not adhere to the DoD parent-fee schedule. Third, we were not always able to collect the information that we needed because of the nature of the contract under which a center operates. The best example of this last point is Vance Air Force Base in Oklahoma, which has a contractor-run center on the installation that caters to military personnel. Vance personnel were not able to provide us with

---

[17]This difference is statistically significant at the 5-percent level.

the cost information we required because child care is just a small part of a much larger base-operating support contract, and it was not possible to isolate the costs related to child care.

Characteristics of the contractor-operated centers are presented in Table 4.15. This table makes it clear that there is enormous diversity in the way in which contracts are written and in the menu of services provided to these centers by the government. Further, there are substantial differences across contractors in the percentage of all children cared for within each center.

Interestingly, the lowest percentages of infants are found in two centers with unique arrangements: One requires that parent fees cover child-care costs; the other subsidizes fees in local community-based centers. In the first case, the percentage of infants who receive services may be low because infant-care costs are high; fees that are not subsidized and are paid directly to the contractor must reflect these high costs. In the second case, there simply may not be very many infant slots available in the centers included in the contract, a situation that is common in community-based centers.

Even in our small sample, we found that contractor-based care is provided through several types of arrangements. One location pays the difference between the DoD fee schedule and the fees at accredited child-care centers in the local area. The DoD does not have a "contract" with any single center, and parents can choose which one they like best. One center operates under a GSA arrangement, whereby the government pays the cost of the facilities (and these costs are explicitly considered in the cost estimate) but the parent fees must cover all other costs.[18] At the other centers, the government provides the contractor with the facilities (these costs are not included in the cost estimate) and subsidizes the cost of providing care by supplementing parent fees; these fees conform to the DoD fee schedule.

_____

[18]This arrangement differs from the one that governs care in DoD CDCs, where a substantial subsidy means that parent fees cover only direct-care costs.

Table 4.15

Characteristics of Contractor-Operated Centers

Contractor Site Enrollment	Percentage of Infants Served	Contract Arrangement	Parent Fees	Services Provided by Government
305	7%	Government contracts with a private company (also the child-care provider) to build CDCs and the DoD pays mortgage, as well as any maintenance and facility upgrade costs	No government subsidy for provision of child care Parent fees paid directly to the child-care contractor Parent board negotiates fees with contractor Fees vary by child age This center is run according to GSA model	Utilities Security Maintenance
82	10%	Government contracts with the child-care provider Contractor gets a fixed amount per child per week; amount varies by child age Government pays difference between parent fee and contracted amount Government pays for most of equipment	Parent fees based on DoD fee schedule and depend on family income, not age of child	Utilities Telephone Maintenance Custodial

Table 4.15 (continued)

Contractor Site Enrollment	Percentage of Infants Served	Contract Arrangement	Parent Fees	Services Provided by Government
133	16% (infants and pre-toddlers)	Government contracts with the child-care provider Contractor gets a fixed amount per child per week Amount is different for enrollments under and over 200 Amount varies by child age Government pays difference between parent fee and contracted amount	Parent fees based on DoD fee schedule and depend on family income, not age of child	Utilities Maintenance Custodial Security Snow removal Background checks Supplies
97	33% (infants and pre-toddlers)	Government contracts with the child-care provider Contractor gets a fixed amount per child per week Government pays difference between parent fee and contracted amount We do not know how fee varies by child age	Parent fees based on DoD fee schedule and depend on family income, not age of child	Utilities Maintenance Security Background checks Supplies
54 (subsidized children at several centers)	4%	Government does not contract with a single provider but subsidizes fees for center-based care at several accredited centers in local area Government pays difference between tuition and parent fees specified by DoD fee schedule	Parent fees based on DoD fee schedule	—

Our cost estimates are based on two cost elements: (1) the costs incurred by the DoD in contracting for child care and (2) parent fees. DoD costs include payments to contractors to supplement parent fees, contract administration costs, other DoD administration, the cost of materials and supplies, and parent fees. In other words, we captured only the resources that flow from the DoD and parents to the contractor, and the costs incurred by the DoD in administering the contract.

In all cases, the contract between the DoD and the contractor had specified fees based on the age of the child served. In most cases, parent fees followed the DoD schedule based on total family income rather than child age. Consequently, the DoD payment to the contractor tended to be higher for younger children whose parents typically are younger and therefore earn less than parents of older children. While our cost estimates do reflect those differential contractor fees, they do not capture any cross-subsidization that might occur within the contractor's organization. In other words, the contractor might experience a loss on each infant but make up for the loss through a profit on each preschool-age child. For this reason, we expect that these cost estimates, while reflective of what the DoD and parents are paying for this care, might underestimate the actual cost the provider incurs in caring for infants and possibly overestimate the actual cost of care for older children.

The survey data reveal that the cost to the DoD and parents of contractor-operated care varies much less by age group than does the cost of DoD-provided care. The difference between the infant costs and preschool-age cost at some locations is essentially zero, and in no case is it greater than $3,000 per year. This contrasts with the DoD-run centers, where the average cost of infant care is over $5,000 per year *more* than the average cost of preschool-age care. As a result, we find that the cost of care for infants in a contractor-operated center is generally lower than the cost of infant care at the average CDC, whereas the cost of preschool-age care in a contractor-run center is much higher than the cost of providing such care in DoD centers.[19] This finding of more-uniform costs across child age in

_____

[19]One should not conclude from this discussion that the DoD could easily meet the need for care of the youngest children most cost effectively by contracting out infant and pre-toddler care. Due to the higher cost of caring for very young children, these

contractor-operated centers may reflect the possibility that contractors are cross-subsidizing infant care with the higher fees from preschool-age care, something that we know goes on in community-based centers (Cost, Quality, and Child Outcomes Study Team, 1995). However, we do not have the data to determine whether this speculation is correct.

The cost estimates we present incorporate the costs incurred by the DoD in administering the contractor-operated center programs. These costs include contract monitoring and administration, background checks in some cases, enrollment management, utilities, maintenance, supplies, training and curriculum specialists, and other attendant costs. As noted in Table 4.16, the costs covered by the government vary from contract to contract. Moreover, in some cases, even when these costs are "covered" by the government as opposed to being covered by the contractor, they don't always appear in the Child Development System (CDS) budget. Reported other costs range from $151 per child to $2,092 per child.

Because of the small sample, we cannot draw any strong conclusions about the cost of contractor-operated care. As with DoD-run care, there is significant variation across sites regarding the indirect costs that are recorded in the CDS budget. However, we note that the cost of contractor-operated care clearly falls within the range of costs observed for DoD-run care. The estimated cost per infant in the contractor-based centers is generally lower than the average cost per

Table 4.16

Estimated Cost Per Child in Contractor-Operated Centers

	Center 1	Center 2	Center 3	Center 4	Center 5[b]
Infant	$9,074	$6,131	$10,386	$9,684	$7,802–$9,362
Pre-toddler	$9,074	$5,559	$9,606	$8,592	$7,802–$8,530
Toddler	$6,162	$5,559	$8,566	$8,332	$6,450–$7,282
Preschool	$6,162	$4,935	$8,566	$7,812	$6,138–$6,814
School-age	$7,098[a]	—	$8,306	—	$4,110–$4,526

[a]Licensed kindergarten.

[b]Because Center 5 consists of multiple accredited centers, a dollar range is shown.

children make up only a small fraction of total enrollment in centers run by private firms. Long waiting lists typically exist for infant and pre-toddler slots.

infant in DoD-run centers, whereas the cost per preschooler in the contractor-based centers is generally higher than the average cost per preschooler in DoD-run centers. There is, therefore, no evidence that contractor-run centers are either cheaper or more expensive than DoD-run centers.[20]

This final observation is important to a discussion of the outsourcing of DoD child care. The rules governing outsourcing in the federal government, set forth in OMB Circular A-76, allow the government to outsource any service that is currently performed by federal employees *only* if it can be demonstrated that a contractor can provide the same quality of service at a cost that is at least 10-percent lower than the government's cost. Our data do not indicate that contractor-provided care is less costly than DoD-run care. Nor can we comment on the quality of care, since we used accreditation as our sole quality criterion. While accreditation establishes that a center meets NAEYC guidelines, there are nevertheless variations in quality across accredited centers.

---

[20]We also emphasize that we did not examine the quality of any of the centers in our study, although we do note that they are all accredited.

Chapter Five

AN EXAMINATION OF CIVILIAN-EMPLOYER CHILD-CARE CENTERS

The military child-care system is by far the country's largest system of employer-sponsored child care and serves the largest percentage of employees. It is also known for the effort and energy the DoD and the Services continuously expend in improving the system and the quality of care the system delivers. Given the DoD's motivation for continuous improvement, we believe that an examination of the ways that other employers, particularly those in the civilian sector, provide child care can offer some useful insights to military planners. In addition, the information we gathered on civilian employers places the data we collected on military child-care costs into a broader context.

Our goal was to highlight how a small number of employers who share the military's goal of providing high-quality, affordable care to the children of their employees have dealt with some key issues that the military has also addressed. These issues include how to decide on an appropriate subsidy level, manage the demand for care, and ensure quality. We also wanted to find out what civilian employers think about the value to their business of providing child care for the children of their employees.

We wanted to gain some insights from firms that operate employer-sponsored child-care centers that are similar in terms of subsidy level and that share the military's concerns about quality. To get a perspective on issues of scale, we also conducted interviews with several large-scale, nationwide contractors that operate centers for some of the employers that are included in our study.

Our requests to visit the civilian centers were met politely but often with puzzlement. We were asked by individuals at several potential civilian employer study sites why people studying the military child-care system would want to interview them, when it is *the military* system that has been widely touted of late as a model for the entire nation. We responded by noting the complexity of our task and the military's desire to continually improve its system. We told individuals at these sites that we were examining military child care within the general context of employer-sponsored care. We further explained that the military was interested in looking at alternative ways to deliver care and believed that it could learn from the experiences of other employers. After hearing our explanation, these employers were very willing to allow us to visit their centers and were open about discussing the rewards and challenges of delivering care to their employees' children. None of the employers we contacted refused to host our visit.

EMPLOYER CHARACTERISTICS

The employers included in this portion of our study vary tremendously in just about every way. Of the seven centers we visited, four are sponsored by private, for-profit employers, while the other three have federal government sponsorship—two have sponsorship from the GSA and the third from the Pentagon, which subsidizes the cost of the center's space and maintenance. The private employers tend to be those whose interest in providing on-site child care is easy to understand: Two are involved in producing items consumed by families—they see their child-care centers as symbols of their commitment to children and families. The other two employers are a high-tech corporation and an advertising agency. Most of these employers became involved in delivering child care on-site out of a perceived need and a sense that the center would provide benefits to both the employees and themselves, and from the wish to be seen as responsive and progressive employers.

The employers we visited are "all over the map"—in large urban office buildings, suburban campuses, and semirural settings. For the four private employers, their centers presented a way to maintain employee loyalty and get "good press" while meeting a need for nearby, high-quality care. The GSA centers, by comparison, seemed to be responding to a real need in the workplace being expressed from the bottom up.

Most of the employers we interviewed generally could be characterized as "employee-sensitive." As shown in Table 5.1, all of the private employers we visited provide their employees with additional lifestyle benefits beside the child-care centers. These employers are willing to put their dollars behind the effort to be sensitive to the needs of employees.

Employer size ranges widely—from an advertising agency with only 70 employees to a firm with 8,500 employees at just one of its multiple sites. Interestingly, the size of the child-care centers bore only a slight relationship to the size of the employers. While the advertising agency had a small center, and the Pentagon center (with a capacity of 202) was one of the largest we visited, the size of the other centers

Table 5.1

Characteristics of Sponsoring Employers

	Number of Employees on Site[a]	Type of Site	Type of Business Enterprise	Other Employee Services
Private Employer 1	3,000	Suburban campus	Private for profit	Gym
Private Employer 2	70	Suburban office building	Private for profit	Gym
Private Employer 3	8,500	Suburban campus	Private for profit	Gym; lactation rooms
Private Employer 4	1,600	Suburban office building	Private for profit	Gym; lactation rooms; lockers
Pentagon	23,000	Urban office building	Federal government	Gym; clinic
GSA Employer 1	642	Urban office building	Federal government	None
GSA Employer 2	708	Semirural campus	Federal government	None

[a]Excludes employees at other locations.

was independent of the size of the workforce.[1] In fact, both of the GSA centers were quite small even though one of them was located in a very large urban office building.

CENTER CHARACTERISTICS

The centers that we visited vary substantially across a number of important dimensions, which are displayed in Table 5.2. Jointly, these ten dimensions define key aspects of each center.

Whether or not a parent board exists is an indicator of the extent to which an employer seeks to involve parents in the development of center policy. In GSA centers, such a board is required, and it plays a larger role in center decisions than do the other parent boards. In particular, GSA parent boards are charged with selecting the contractor that will operate the center.

Staff-to-child ratios are a key indicator of quality. To simplify the comparison, we limit the presentation to a staff-to-infant ratio.

Who the operator is defines to some extent how the center operates: If the operator is a large nationwide company under contract to the employer, one can assume that formal policies, regional oversight, and child-care experience exists. If the employer operates the center, it is more likely that the center reflects the company's view of how to best operate a child-care center.

Whether or not a sliding scale is in place provides some insight on the employer's views concerning access to care.

Sick-child care is a benefit that some employers provide, usually at a separate site. This dimension suggests a fairly high level of financial commitment to child care. Sick-child care generally is costly because it may not be used on a regular basis but must be staffed with at least a few individuals with some medical training.

---

[1] The Pentagon is not a military installation; therefore, the CDC at the Pentagon is not under DoD control.

Table 5.2

Characteristics of Visited Centers

	Parent Board?	Staff/Child Ratios (Infants)	Operator	Sliding Scale?	Employer-Sponsored Sick-Child Care?	Total Center Capacity	Monthly Infant Fee[a]	Employer-Specific Openings?	Hours of Operation	Accredited?
Private-Employer Center 1	No	1:3	Bright Horizons	Yes: four levels	Yes: off-site shared center	100	$933/ $782/ $649; includes lunch and snacks; $25 monthly diaper fee	"Gift Night" one time per year	7 a.m.– 7 p.m.	Yes
Private-Employer Center 2	No	1:3	Employer	Yes	No, but employer pays for supplemental care	23	$440– $880; includes lunch	None	8 a.m.– 6:30 p.m.; shorter hours and full employee benefits help in staff recruitment	Beginning the process

Table 5.2 (continued)

	Parent Board?	Staff/ Child Ratios (Infants)	Operator	Sliding Scale?	Employer-Sponsored Sick-Child Care?	Total Center Cap- acity	Monthly Infant Fee[a]	Employer-Specific Openings?	Hours of Operation	Accred- ited?
Private-Employer Center 3	Yes	1:3	Knowl-edge Learning Centers	No	No	204	$790; tuition (lunch and snacks included) must cover staff salaries	"Parents Night Out" two times per year	6:30 a.m–6:30 p.m.	Yes
Private-Employer Center 4	No	1:3	Bright Horizons	No	No	88	$785; staff salaries absorb 110 percent of fee revenue; lunch and snacks included	Annual trade show: for two weeks open until 9 p.m.; employer covers additional costs	6:45 a.m–6:45 p.m.	Yes

Table 5.2 (continued)

	Parent Board?	Staff/Child Ratios (Infants)	Operator	Sliding Scale?	Employer-Sponsored Sick-Child Care?	Total Center Capacity	Monthly Infant Fee[a]	Employer-Specific Openings?	Hours of Operation	Accredited?
Pentagon Center	Yes	1:4	Aramark	No	No	202	$774	None	6:30 a.m.–6 p.m.	Yes
GSA-Employer Center 1	Yes (required)	1:4	National Pediatric Support Services, Inc.	No	No	53	$725; tuition covers staff costs and supplies; excludes food	None	6:45 a.m.–6 p.m.	Yes
GSA-Employer Center 2	Yes (required)	1:3	Parent Board	No	No	55	$703;[b] tuition must cover staff costs	None	7:30 a.m.–6 p.m.	Yes

[a] At some child-care centers, center employees may purchase care for their own children at much-reduced rates. Those reduced rates are not listed here.

[b] Fee for federal employees. Nonfederal parents pay a higher sum.

Total center capacity provides a quick measure of scope, and when compared with the number of employees on site (see Table 5.1), it may be suggestive of the availability of care.

The monthly infant fee is a shorthand way of comparing centers and understanding how that subsidy is used—whether it goes to reduce parent fees or to increase center resources (of course, employee populations vary in their capacity to pay; this may be a major factor in how those fees are set).

Employer-specific "openings" are those times when the center is open beyond regular hours. We collected those data because we imagined that this might be a case when an employer derives some clear benefits from having an on-site center. For instance, one center extended its hours while employees prepared for a yearly industry trade show.

Hours of operation indicate how long the center is open each day. Of particular note is whether the operating hours allow some flexibility for parents in their working hours.

Whether or not a center is accredited is generally regarded as one index of the quality of care.

We had also hoped to calculate a subsidy level for each center but were unable to do so because of lack of access to the necessary data.

In the following subsections, we discuss these dimensions in more detail.

Management of the Center

This center characteristic depends upon whether an outside contractor runs the center or the employer runs the center directly. In the latter case, child-care center staffers are company employees; they typically receive the same benefits as other employees, which makes the position more attractive to potential staff.

By nature of our selection process, five of the seven centers we visited are operated by a total of four contractors (one company in our sample operates two centers). Each of the contractors is an experienced provider of child care, both on a contract basis with employers and as an operator of community-based centers. According to the employers' representatives, the decision to bring in a child-care operator was an easy one to make; the option of running the child-care center themselves was never considered.

Interestingly, in the case of the single employer-run center in our study (the child-care staffers are company employees receiving the same benefits as other employees), the decision to run the center was never formally made. The center simply grew out of efforts by the company founders, a married couple, to deal with their own need for care for their children. For reasons of equity, the founders decided that others should also be able to bring their infants to the work site as they had done and receive care for them on-site. Over time, an informal effort developed into an established center.

The employers who hired outside contractors to operate their centers did so for two reasons. First, the employers did not want to be diverted from their core business to take on the operation of a child-care center. Second, the employers wanted to create some distance between themselves and the centers. An HR person at one of these employers said, "We made the outsourcing decision because others are more knowledgeable [about the child-care business] and we didn't want to assume the liability." However, according to a representative of one of the management companies we interviewed, any reduction in liability is illusory: "The employer is always liable even if there is an operator in there. If someone sues, they will go after the operator but will also go after the employer. The major benefit of bringing in an operator is that the corporation doesn't have to deal with day-to-day issues, such as an incident when one child bites another."

For all employers who contracted out care, doing so meant that employees were less likely to call HR with questions about center policies, or to express their dissatisfaction with their position on a waiting list, or to complain about the way a particular incident at the center was handled. One HR representative said, "Care-center operators are professionals. Their procedures are informed by their knowledge of children. It's not just [an employer] coming up with some arbitrary policy."

None of the employers we interviewed expected that outsourcing would save them money. Most noted that the company managing the center needs to make a profit, and this profit must be included in the employer's costs. Sometimes, the costs associated with contracting out center management to a large national operator can be reduced somewhat by the savings gained through regional management and use of a standard curriculum, in which case, costs are amortized across many centers. Said one HR person, "[The company] never thought that we would save costs by contracting out. We made the outsourcing decision for other reasons." The administrator of a management company echoed this view: "Outsourcing may not result in any real financial savings to the employer."

Even if employers cannot avoid liability, it certainly seems that they can place some distance between themselves and the provision of care by engaging a professional child-care center operator. The director of the one employer-run center we visited told us that she often has to address complaints about policies that go unquestioned in the professionally managed centers. For example, that center, like many others, has a policy that heavily penalizes parents who are late in picking up their children at closing time (in this case, the charge is $1 per minute). Company employees frequently protest the policy, arguing, for instance, that it is not their fault that their boss who works in the same building keeps them past closing time.

Employing an outside contractor that runs multiple centers benefited caregivers in important ways. In some cases, because of the large numbers served by the contractors, caregivers were enrolled in benefit plans that were more generous than if the contractor had run just a single center. In the case of one contractor, its national focus allowed caregivers to receive promotions within the company that might not otherwise be possible, which also increased retention.[2]

In several cases, involvement with a multicenter contractor also reduced the costs associated with curriculum design and implementation. The contractor in these cases provided a curriculum that was used in multiple centers, so the cost of developing the curriculum

---

[2]Although, moving from lead teacher to assistant director, for instance, might mean that a particular caregiver would leave a given center, such a move would not count as turnover.

was amortized over more than one center. This approach, however, was criticized by one of the higher-end center operators to whom we spoke. In the view of that operator, one of the things that keeps caregivers fresh and responsive to a child's needs are that the curriculum and programs are geared to the local community. Standardizing a curriculum leads to less parent and child satisfaction and more staff turnover because staff members may feel that they have little or no choice in what they offer to children.

Several contractors provided regionalized oversight systems, in which a regional administrator is responsible for the quality and safety of a number of centers in a geographic area. A staff member in one organization that uses this approach argued that an administrative system such as this allows quality-monitoring procedures to be conducted at less cost to the center. It also provides a mechanism for preserving and disseminating information about successful care practices or management techniques. In addition, regional administration enables a staffer to travel to a given center promptly if his or her presence is urgently needed.

In all cases, center directors told us that they valued having a large organization behind them. One director, who had lengthy experience running a community-based center in a church, told us that having a well-known, well-regarded operator behind her provided a "measure of comfort" that was lacking when she was running a center on her own.

The administrator for one of the care-center management companies noted another benefit of bringing in a management company: It is relatively easy to replace that company if the employer becomes dissatisfied or wants to change its program. "They know that they can fire us at any time," the administrator said. "Companies really like that aspect." Interestingly, no center director or HR person brought this up as an advantage to using an outside contractor, probably because there had been no turnover in care-center management companies except at one of the GSA centers. In that case, the turnover had been relatively uneventful.

Costs and Cost Sharing

This dimension of center characteristics involves the nature of the subsidy provided by the employer to the center. When an employer determines that it will provide on-site child care, it is generally understood that this provision will not be a break-even undertaking. Indeed, a key characteristic of employer-sponsored child care is the subsidy that flows from the employer to the child-care center. Employers provide such subsidies for many reasons, including polishing their image as a family-friendly company, reducing absenteeism and turnover, and aiding recruitment. Providing such a subsidy raises complex issues for an employer. The fact that this subsidy will actually be enjoyed by only a small number of families could become an issue. Moreover, as employees without children have become more vocal about the inequity they perceive in the provision of benefits, the fact that the child-care subsidy goes only to employees with children could be a sensitive issue (Belkin, 2000).

Given that a subsidy will be provided, a number of questions arise: How much should it be? On what basis should it be provided? Should the same level of subsidy be provided to every family who uses the center? Or should those families earning less receive more?

The levels of subsidy provided to the centers we visited ranged widely. Interestingly, not all employers were able or willing to provide us with an exact number. Although in the minority, these employers essentially believed that they had made a commitment to high-quality care and were prepared to spend as much as it took to deliver it. At the more-modest end, in terms of subsidy levels, the two GSA centers provided a building and its utilities and maintenance, and little else.

The GSA does have some funds available for purchases of major equipment designed to last more than one year, and in recent years has been able to fund most of the items on its 113 centers' lists of necessities. Indeed, the GSA has been encouraging its centers to think bigger by urging them to buy higher-quality equipment that will last longer rather than buying the cheapest version of whatever they need. The GSA has also taken to buying critical items in bulk, such as latex gloves for diaper changing, which enables the GSA to obtain these items at considerably lower cost. This is one approach to subsidy that builds on the enormous size and buying power of federal agencies. In addition, one of the two GSA centers we visited receives some in-kind support from its own federal agency in the form of office supplies and furniture from the agency's warehouse. Overall, subsidies from private employers are more generous than subsidies from the government, although most employers do attempt to keep subsidies under control.

All employers subsidizing child care for employees face the competing objectives of controlling costs, ensuring quality, and providing widespread access to care. Many private-sector employers have decided to sacrifice the goal of widespread access in the interest of cost control and maintenance of quality. This is quite different from the DoD's emphasis on access.

Of course, there are ways to control costs without sacrificing quality or accessibility. One employer, for example, creates a supplies fund each year that the center director can use to purchase whatever items are needed. The employer also provides ongoing staff training and development plus an independent consultant on health and safety. This, in addition to the facility and its maintenance, constitutes the full subsidy. Along with this subsidy, this employer requires that fees be set so that they cover personnel costs, something that would obviously have to happen anyway if the subsidy fund could only be used for supplies. Initial fees were set at a level that made them affordable to the mid-level worker. In an effort to keep fees affordable, fee increases must be approved by the employer and are linked to the average wage increase for that year. This employer's HR staff told us that the employer has made it clear to the child-care center management company that the employer will not "bail out" the center if the management company has difficulty operating within the constraints just outlined. What this means, of course, is that in running the center, the management company assumes the risk that it may receive no profit whatsoever if expenses exceed the combination of parent fees and subsidy.

Some of the more-generous, profit-generating employers provided more-generous subsidies to their centers. In one case, the center has been given carte blanche to use the employer's support systems, including photocopying and ordering of supplies. This means that the supply budget, which is agreed upon each year, can be dedicated to the purchase of child-care related items not available in the corporate stores. Another employer, as we were told by the center director, "was going for a showpiece." Consequently, there was virtually no ceiling on expenses. The director of this center also said that, with regard to operating costs, the center has never been questioned. This latter employer is one with "deep pockets" and interviewees at every site made it clear to us that they were definitely not in that category.

In addition to the issue of generosity in providing a subsidy, there is also the issue of risk. In the case of both of the centers just mentioned, the contract with the employer is a "cost plus fee" arrangement. The employer covers the difference between parent fees and operating costs, and also awards the contractor a management fee (profit). Under such an arrangement, the employer, rather than the contractor, assumes all the risk. If costs are higher than expected, the employer pays more.[3]

The issue of risk is a particularly salient one with the GSA centers, according to GSA staff. As noted earlier, the federal subsidy is limited to the building and its maintenance (with an annual equipment fund of an unknown size); the GSA does not guarantee management fees to the management company. Consequently, said one GSA staffer, "This practically guarantees that the first year of operation will be a loss to the company, since there are so many things that have to be worked out." Naturally, this situation limits the pool of firms interested in managing a GSA center, the staffer further noted.

At all employer-sponsored centers we visited, costs are shared among employers and parents. As a result, the key questions are: How much will the parents pay, how much will the employer pay, and is that total enough to cover the cost of providing care? As revealed in Chapter Four in the analysis of costs at DoD-run centers, the labor cost for child-care providers represents a large proportion (between 50 and 80 percent) of the total cost of providing care. This reality presents significant challenges to employers. Attempts to reduce the amount paid to the contractor will likely reduce wages paid

---

[3]Much attention is paid to the issue of risk assumption and cost containment in the DoD. But our civilian center visits make it clear that these concerns are not unique to the military.

to caregivers.[4] At the same time, even when caregivers earn low wages and the employer covers the cost of the facility and its maintenance, some employees still cannot afford the cost of care, particularly if the center is providing high-quality care (defined as meeting adult-to-child ratio levels advocated by the NAEYC).

Centers and employers have dealt with these challenges very differently and therefore set their fees quite differently. One employer very consciously sets parent fees (in consultation with the center director) so that the "average" employee can afford to have one child in the center. In this case, because the employer does not guarantee the management company a fee, this decision leaves the management company to figure out how to comply with the fee structure and run the center according to agreed-upon criteria (one of which is that the center be accredited), and still come out with a reasonable return on its investment.

In the for-profit employer centers, employers have attempted to minimize the situation of parents being subsidized through low wages paid to center staff by subsidizing the center staff wages themselves. This has had the effect of increasing caregiver wages and reducing turnover, while keeping parent fees affordable, at least for those employees who are able to acquire a slot at the center.

In the case of some GSA centers, affordability has become a significant issue. The GSA generally looks for four elements to be in place before it decides that a work site is appropriate for a center. First, both employees and management must express interest in having a center. Second, there must be an appropriate space. Third, there must be a large enough employee base to support a center (the GSA has found that 3 to 5 percent of employees wind up using the center). And, finally, the average government service (GS) scale (pay grade) must be high enough for employees to be able to afford the center fees.

---

[4]Recent research suggests that caregivers are paid substantially less than people with similar skills and training working outside of the child-care field. By working for below-market wages, caregivers essentially subsidize parents (Cost, Quality, and Child Outcomes Study Team, 1995; Campbell et al., 2000).

But this approach doesn't always work. Said a GSA staffer, "Politics dominate in some places." She described a site in which the first three elements checked out, but the average GS level was so low that it was clear affordability would be a huge issue. But employees at this site, which has a largely minority workforce, felt strongly about having a center and higher-ups did not want to appear to discriminate against their employees by denying them a child-care center. The GSA proceeded, even though its child-care staff knew they were literally constructing a problem for themselves. The center was built and was undersubscribed. Bad feelings were created because fees, which had to cover all costs except facility expenses, were so high that many employees could not afford them. For the GSA, there was no obvious solution. Unlike the private employers we visited, the GSA could not step in to subsidize fees in order to reduce them. This sort of situation was mentioned by an HR person who works for one of the for-profit companies that employs a highly educated workforce, most of whom can afford the fees. "Our fees [in our center] are market-based," said the HR representative, "but in some industries the employees couldn't afford to use the center."

A bill was recently passed that could be helpful to federal employees who find that they are unable to pay center fees. Legislation passed in 1999, which was good for one year and potentially renewable, provided a pilot tuition subsidy program to help federal employees cover child-care costs.[5] Employees of agencies that have expressed a willingness to participate in the program may receive a subsidy for child-care expenses based on ability to pay.

As of October 2000, the GSA Child Care Subsidy Assistance Plan had developed a benefit schedule that considers a family's AGI and the number of children in the family eligible for care. For families with less than $35,000 in AGI and one child, the GSA subsidy will cover annual child-care expenses that exceed 5 percent of AGI ($1,750). According to this schedule, families with more children in care must

---

[5]Public Law 106-58, Section 643, is designed to help low-income federal employees access affordable child care. It authorizes federal agencies to use appropriated funds ("otherwise available to such agencies for salaries") to subsidize child-care services. This legislation was targeted at other federal agencies that did not already have authority to use appropriated funds in this way. The DoD, as executive agent, has opted not to implement this discretionary authority because it already had in place a child development system, funded partially through appropriated funds.

spend a larger percentage of their income on child care, but they also get a larger subsidy. Families with an AGI between $35,000 and $51,500 are also eligible for GSA subsidies, but must pay more out of their own pockets before they become eligible for the subsidy. For example, a family with an AGI of $40,000 and one child can receive a subsidy on expenditures exceeding 6.43 percent of AGI ($2,572). For a family with an AGI of $50,000 and one child, the subsidy only covers expenditures over 25.25 percent of AGI ($12,625).

The GSA has also instituted parent boards at each of its centers. Each parent board can become a nonprofit board of directors after applying for 501(c)(3) tax-exempt status. The board issues an RFP (request for proposal) to select a management company, with the GSA retaining veto power over this decision. According to GSA staff, the key purpose of these boards is to raise money so that parents in need can receive tuition assistance. However, according to GSA staff members, these boards often resist the idea of raising funds because most board members do not need such assistance. The GSA expects boards to develop a fundraising plan, which may include teaming up with the Combined Federal Campaign[6] run by the Office of Personnel Management. Currently, recycling refunds can be used for tuition assistance, which benefits boards and centers.

Private employers have tried a number of ways to manage parent fees. Two of the employers whose centers we visited have instituted sliding scales for parent fees based on ability to pay. In one of those centers, parents must submit the previous year's tax returns in order to avoid paying the highest fees. In the one employer-managed center we visited, this policy has created tension. Employees eventually find out who is paying more and who is paying less, and have expressed resentment toward those who pay less.

Turning back to Table 5.2, what is perhaps most striking about the fees for these centers is how considerable they are, given the nontrivial levels of subsidization in every case. In all of the centers except one, the monthly cost for an infant (each of these centers levies fees that vary with child age) exceeds $700 per month (using the

---

[6]Agencies conduct this campaign annually to raise money from federal employees for nonprofit organizations. The GSA recommends that boards team up with this activity to raise money for their centers.

midrange fee in those centers that have a sliding scale). This dollar figure, according to one HR person, is nevertheless below the market rate in the Los Angeles area, for example. Even in the GSA center that requires parents to contribute substantial time each week as part of its cooperative policy in order to keep staffing costs lower, the monthly fee for infants is more than $700. Moreover, these fees are remarkably similar across centers nationwide. This probably reflects efforts on the part of most centers to base their fees on an annual fee survey and phone calls made to similar centers to find out what they are charging.

The relatively high infant-fee level reflects a decision made by every employer to set fees on the basis of child age so that fees roughly reflect the actual costs of care. However, one interviewee noted that the cost of providing care for infants is many times greater than the cost of providing care for older children. The fee structure by child age in every center we visited does not come close to reflecting the magnitude of the disparity between the cost of care for infants and that for older children. Said one HR person, "The infants are a major cost-loser; we make up for it with the preschoolers."

A policy that charges parents of infants more than parents of older children seemed only fair to our interviewees. All of them rejected the idea of a single fee or sliding scale that ignored a child's age. Said one HR person, "Our salaries are comparable in the infant and preschool classrooms, but we are paying out a lot more to care for each infant, and there is no way that the actual costs of care are picked up in the ($700 per month) infant fee." Said one care-center management company staffer, "Parents need to recognize that it costs much more to take care of an infant."

The high infant-fee level is also significant because of the heavy subsidization of these centers. Even the least-subsidized centers are given space and maintenance without charge. According to all our respondents, the infant-fee level simply reflects just how much high-quality care costs. Interviewees whose organizations manage both employer-sponsored and community-based (unsubsidized) centers note that employer sponsorship is, as one of our interviewees said, a "godsend." Said another interviewee, "A lot depends on the cost of rent in community-based centers. It is so difficult to keep community-based centers afloat. Employer-supported centers have better equipment, salaries are higher, and you can offer higher-quality programs."

Indeed, the managers of less-heavily subsidized centers noted that even with the rent and maintenance covered, it isn't easy to provide the high-quality care they strive for within their fee structure. For the most part, these centers manage to provide quality care by doing five things. First, they staff on the high side of allowable child-to-staff ratios (for example, a four-to-one ratio for infants rather than the three-to-one ratio used in the most-heavily subsidized centers). Second, they pay their staff less. As one interviewee well acquainted with child-care centers noted, the big costs are in staffing. If staff can be hired for less money, the difference really adds up. Third, they minimize staff benefits. Fourth, they limit administrative positions. For example, a national provider that we interviewed noted that such things as curriculum design and monitoring are regionalized to save funds. Fifth, they keep close tabs on incidental costs. As the head of one management organization said, "We essentially have to adopt a 'no waste' policy, particularly in unsubsidized centers. This means that we *will* deny a request for a ream of paper if the director has exceeded his or her materials costs, which run about $4.50 per child per month."

CENTER PROGRAMS AND FEATURES

All of the centers we visited, except the employer-run center, were currently accredited (the managers of the employer-run center were just beginning the self-study process during our visit and hoped to become accredited in the near future). Each center, accredited or not, meets NAEYC guidelines with regard to child-to-staff ratios and several even improve upon them. Although there are substantial differences in how the programs are run, and in the availability of human resources and resources of other sorts, it is fair to say that these centers all provide high-quality care, based on a national (NAEYC) standard.

Because the purpose of our visits was not to comment on the individual centers but to contextualize our understanding of military child care as employer-sponsored care, we focused on those aspects of the centers' programs that are most important for an employer-sponsored center. Our focus in this section covers three areas: general quality, unique employer needs that are met through program accommodations, and aspects of a program that may put an employer's needs before those of a family.

General Quality

As we noted earlier, all the centers we visited were high-quality centers based on their accreditation status (all but one is currently accredited). But quality can, of course, vary among accredited centers; there were substantial variations across centers on dimensions associated with quality, such as child-to-staff ratios and staff turnover.[7] We found that child-to-staff ratios in these centers were lower than what the NAEYC suggests.

Interviews with staff of the management companies underscored the enormous value of employer subsidies in enabling centers to provide high-quality care. This view is supported by the findings of the Cost, Quality, and Child Outcomes Study (1995), which showed that the worksite centers in the study sample were providing higher-quality care than the unsubsidized centers. The higher quality was attributed to the centers' being less reliant on parent fees because of funds from other sources. These funds were used to increase staff salaries and benefits, improve child-to-staff ratios, and hire better-qualified staff. Indeed, the RAND research team was impressed by the level of quality and stuck by the relatively high fees necessary to achieve that quality, given that in every case the center was operating rent free and maintenance free.

Employer Motivations, Rewards, and Costs

The nongovernment employers to whom we spoke were clear about the reasons that they had chosen to sponsor on-site child care. For most, the center represented a tool that would convey an important message about the company—that it was family friendly and a place that cares about its employees. As one HR person said, the center

---

[7]As one would expect, those centers with better-paid staff tended to have lower turnover.

"sends a message about the culture of the company." That message is a very positive one, and, the company believes, attracts staff.

An HR staffer for another employer said virtually the same thing about his company's center: "We want this center to be a showplace for people. Lots of important people come through our company, including senior dignitaries, congressmen, and members of the British parliament."

At one center, we were told a story that obviously resonated powerfully among the staff. Some years ago, the company was trying to lure a high-level executive away from a competitor. The usual enticements had been dangled before this executive, such as stock options and a generous salary, but he was not budging. "Tell me what else you can do for me," he said. Someone remembered that he and his wife had just had a baby. A tour of the company's child-care center was hastily arranged. The recruit was extremely impressed, even when it was made clear that matriculation was not a perquisite that could be provided to him, as enrollments were accepted on a first-come, first-served basis.[8] Despite the fact that care-center enrollment was not offered, he was so impressed with the center that he agreed to accept the company's offer.

The desire to project an image of a family-friendly, concerned employer was manifested in other ways at a number of these companies. Several companies provided workout facilities. One offered insurance coverage to employees' domestic partners (including those of the same gender), then decided to go even further with available coverage. The company now covers one person in addition to the employee. According to the company's HR manager, if an aging parent lives with the employee and the employee takes care of that parent, the parent can be eligible for "extended family member" benefits. Another company has contracted for slots in a center for mildly ill children; each employee has up to two weeks per year of care available in that center.

---

[8]All of the centers we visited had waiting lists. We were assured in each case that acceptance into the center was not based on rank in the company but on when a family asked to be put on the waiting list.

Despite the motivation to appear family-friendly, none of the employers to whom we spoke had seriously considered child-care options other than a care center. Most were reported to be nervous about family child care, given the lack of control over what goes on in an FCC home (which echoes feedback heard from military personnel on this topic, as reported in Zellman and Johansen, 1995). The low profile of FCC certainly would not have provided these employers with the family-friendly image that their well-equipped centers provided to them.

When asked, a few employers did note that they had considered the essential unfairness of their current child-care arrangement—huge subsidies for the lucky few families whose children are enrolled in the center and no help at all for the many others who tried to get in but couldn't be accommodated, or who couldn't afford the tuition so they had to look elsewhere. One HR person told us, "We struggle with that [the inequity inherent in providing a heavily subsidized, small center] because we do provide all these dollars for [a small number of] kids and even fewer families. But we could not afford a voucher program to cover all these parents." The HR person added that everyone can pay for child care pre-tax through a flexible spending account—a benefit that all the participating employers provide.

A point not noted by our respondents, but one that is important, is that an employer-sponsored center increases the supply of child care within a community. Particularly in places where an employer commits to providing the type of care that is the most difficult to find and costly—infant care—the employer-sponsored center can be a real help. The center also provides many parents, whether or not their children are enrolled, with an example of a high-quality center. The employer is not only demonstrating its values by communicating to employees that high-quality care is important to the employer, it also provides parents with something that is not always easy to find: an example of what high-quality care looks like.

Several employers noted that a child-care center can also be a powerful employee-retention device, especially for the small number of families who are using the center at a given time. For those employees, a decision to leave the company means that they are forcing their child to change child-care providers. Further, for any new job to be appealing, it would have to more than match the current salary to compensate for the loss of the nontrivial subsidy represented by the center.

For the most part, representatives of the employers that were involved in this study did not report any serious problems with two key segments of their workforce: employees who applied to the center but who could not be accommodated, and employees without children who might resent that money was going to the center for the small number of families using it. This does not mean that employees didn't notice what is going on. But, as one HR manager said, "We don't hear complaints about how this is something the single folks don't use. We do get complaints that the waiting list is too long."

One of the costs of running a center may be found in the time required on the part of the company employee or employees who are the designated liaisons to the center. We asked each HR person we interviewed how much of his or her time was devoted to the center. Most indicated that it wasn't more than an hour or so a week, and that overseeing the center was just one of numerous responsibilities. In many cases, the HR person's job included overseeing all employee benefits; the center was used by only a small number of employees and represented just one benefit in a substantial portfolio of benefits.

It was clear, though, that these HR people did not keep careful records of the time they did spend on center-related activities. This became apparent in the course of one interview during which an HR person initially told us that she spent no more than an hour a week on center-related activities. Later in the interview, she told us that she was in e-mail contact with the center daily and sometimes three or four times a day. Further, she noted, there was a regularly scheduled in-person meeting every two weeks to keep her current on emerging issues and needs. When we noted the apparent discrepancy between the amount of time she said she allocated to the center and the activities in which she was engaged on a regular basis, she agreed that she did probably spend more than one hour each week on the center. It was our sense that center oversight is fairly time-consuming. But, for most, the amount of time spent on oversight had declined precipitously over the years as the centers became established (for instance, the first "biting" incident or the first time a bigwig had been denied a space had been handled). In thinking through the hours they spend on center-related activities, the HR people tended to pick a small number, which reflected the fact that the center was no longer a problem for them and, for some, had even become a source of deep satisfaction.

Interestingly, a few of the centers had begun to provide additional services, but they were more focused on making the balance between work and family easier for employees and not on meeting employer needs. One center, for example, provides a hot take-out dinner once a month for employees when they come to pick up their children. Said the director of this center, "That is one less night a month when the parents have to rush home to make dinner." Another center hosts a "gift night" once a year before Christmas so that parents can shop for holiday gifts while their children are being cared for at the center. This extra service is provided to parents at no additional charge.

Program Accommodations to Meet Employer Needs

One of the reasons that an employer might want to provide on-site child care is that the care can be delivered in a manner that meets unique employer needs. For example, if in the surrounding community there is plenty of care for older children but a dearth of care for infants, an employer might want to make only infant care available.[9] Or, an employer in a community with an adequate amount of child care may want to provide only short-term supplemental (including mildly ill) care, which would enable employees to come to work when their normal child-care arrangements were not available.

Some employers or industries have unique work schedules or operating hours that typical child-care facilities cannot be expected to accommodate. For example, one of the employers included in this study must prepare product for a yearly fair. During the two weeks leading up to the fair, employees put in many additional hours to be ready on time. During those two weeks, the employer keeps the on-site center open until 9 p.m. each evening; the extended-hours costs are picked up by the employer. According to the center director and

---

[9]One of the employers in this study considered doing just that but was advised against it. The employer was told that infant programs, by their nature, have a very limited tenure for parents; although initially thrilled at the prospect of infant care, parents often wind up unhappy when they must leave the center and seek other care within a short period of time.

an HR staffer, these extended hours reduce employee stress and also enable employees to work straight through their shifts without having to leave to pick up their children from regular care and drop them off for whatever evening care parents can arrange.

Interestingly, this was the only example of employer-tailored care that we found. It may be because the other employers do not have such an obvious deadline-driven need. Nevertheless, the director of another center told us that she often gets requests to keep the center open later so employees can work later, but these requests are sporadic and do not justify keeping the center open for extended hours.

These observations are consistent with what Zellman and Johansen (1995) found in their first study of military child care. Despite demands on employees that often include night and weekend work, the military CDCs rarely attempt to accommodate those individual needs. Most directors noted that keeping centers open for extended hours to accommodate individual needs or preferences is virtually never financially justifiable, given that only a small number of families wind up taking advantage of extended-hours care. They note that family child care is much better able to meet such needs. However, CDCs do adjust their hours of operation in response to mission-related needs. For example, at the beginning of the Persian Gulf War, a Marine Corps base kept the CDC open long hours so that employees could prepare for imminent departure to the Gulf.

CONCLUSIONS

Our visits to the civilian child-care centers brought home quite forcefully the central reality of providing child care: It is an extremely costly endeavor. Most of the employers we interviewed were aware of this fact but, for a variety reasons, felt that their companies were ready to assume the considerable cost. One employer that had "backed into" providing child care noted that, in retrospect, a decision to provide care to the children of company employees is a huge and costly decision that should not be made lightly. Nor, said another employer, is it a decision that can easily be reversed down the road. An employer that decides to provide on-site child care has made a serious, long-term, and expensive commitment.

The costliness of on-site child care is revealed in the fairly high fees given the fairly high subsidies. With rent and maintenance covered in every case, and additional subsidies provided in most cases, the parents of infants nevertheless paid more than $700 per month for accredited care in every one of the centers we visited.[10] Fees were high even in those centers with generous subsidies because of a decision to charge fees that were close to the market level to those who could afford to pay them and then use the extra money to improve child-to-staff ratios, increase staff salaries, and in other ways increase the quality of care provided. These fees made it clear just how far unsubsidized centers have to go to stretch a dollar, and how much these centers (and the children) must give up so that they can provide high-quality care while covering the rent and maintenance themselves.

Our findings make it clear that, as a society, we know how to provide high-quality care; it is a lack of funds that stands in the way of being able to do so in many cases. Some parents may be unable to pay enough to get high-quality child care (see Schulman, 2000, for example), or parents or employers may lack the will to devote funds to ensure high-quality care. The availability of an employer subsidy can be, in the words of one of our interviewees, a "godsend." It allows people who could not otherwise afford high-quality care both ready access to that care and the ability to pay for it. The same $700 tuition to employer-supported centers would not provide nearly the same quality of care at a community-based center. Said one management company staffer whose firm operates both subsidized and unsubsidized centers, "Employer-supported centers have better equipment, salaries are higher, and you can provide higher-quality programs." Indeed, the Colorado Cost, Quality, and Child Outcomes Study (1995) found that worksite centers tend to be of higher quality because they are less dependent on parent fees and are able to spend more money on items that increase quality, such as staff wages.

---

[10]One management company staffer told us that the true cost of infant care was actually higher, around $1,200 per month. One contractor noted that California families have the option of hiring relatively cheap immigrant nannies, so that most California centers cannot charge $1,200 a month for infant care and stay in business. She told us that in the Boston area, for example, the cost of living is more or less equivalent to that in Southern California, but because immigrant nannies are not as plentiful, parents are paying $1,200 a month for high-quality infant care.

But, supplying a building, and the utilities and maintenance to go with it, is not always enough. Said one GSA staffer, "If the government paid just a little bit more, it could make a huge difference in terms of affordability of care for lower-level employees."[11]

Our visits brought into sharp focus the astounding ambitiousness of the DoD's worldwide system of child care. The employers we visited typically were running a single center; by comparison, the GSA runs a total of 113 centers around the country. But that pales in comparison to the DoD's hundreds of CDCs and thousands of FCC homes. The employers we interviewed were helping perhaps up to 60 or 100 families, and in the case of the GSA more than 8,000 families. But these numbers are dwarfed by the numbers associated with DoD child care. Moreover, the decision of employers we visited to avoid FCC because of its limited tractability made the DoD's decision to pursue FCC as a means of providing additional and more-flexible care seem even more bold and ambitious. Nowhere else in this country is there an employer system with a goal of providing high-quality child care at an affordable price to almost all employees who need it.

---

[11]The 1985 Trible Amendment (40 U.S.C. 490b) allows federal agencies to give child-care providers rent-free building space and to provide services such as lighting, heating, cooling, electricity, office furniture, office machines and equipment, telephone service, and security systems at no cost. No other federal expenditures were authorized under this amendment. Agencies must ensure that building space is available, and that child-care providers place a priority on serving federal employees. The GSA now provides subsidies for their low-income employees under the authorization of Public Law 106-58, Section 643.

Chapter Six

CONCLUSIONS AND RECOMMENDATIONS

Child care is costly, and those costs are higher for younger children. The fact that child care is expensive to provide is not surprising. Because young children require a great deal of attention from adults, only small numbers of children can be attended to by any one adult (child-to-staff ratios specify the parameters of this level of attention). Within child-care centers, direct-care costs account for a large proportion of the total costs of providing child care (about 50 percent for preschool care and nearly 80 percent for infant care). Indeed, child-care cost studies find labor costs accounting for 70 to 75 percent of the total expended costs (Cost, Quality, and Child Outcomes Study Team, 1995; GAO, 1999).

Because accredited care and safety requirements demand that centers meet minimum staffing ratios, there are limited ways to reduce the costs of accredited care.[1] Consequently, the cost of the caregiver's salary (or in the case of FCC, the caregiver's compensation) must be shared by the relatively small number of children for whom he or she provides care. While it is certainly true that caregivers are not well paid and contribute to lower costs through foregone wages (Cost, Quality, and Child Outcomes Study Team, 1995), they don't work for free. Once caregiver salaries are factored in, child care cannot be provided inexpensively.

At the same time, the incremental cost of high-quality care over mediocre or poor-quality care is quite small. The Cost, Quality, and

---

[1]For example, for the youngest children, staff-to-child ratios are driven by the number of children each staff member can evacuate quickly in the event of an emergency.

Child Outcomes Study Team found, for example, that the mean difference between the cost of care in mediocre-quality centers and the cost of care in developmentally appropriate centers was 25 cents per child hour across a multistate sample. In a related study, Mocan (1997) estimated that the cost of raising a center's quality level from mediocre to the lowest level deemed developmentally appropriate would increase total variable costs 12 cents per hour per child, or 7.5 percent of the center's total costs.

What we know about the benefits of high-quality care to children suggests that providing high-quality care is a very good investment, particularly in light of the small incremental cost involved. The Colorado study and others found that children's cognitive and social development is positively related to the quality of their child-care experience.

Our work also makes clear that costs vary substantially by child age. This is hardly a surprising finding, given that child-to-staff ratios change dramatically as a child matures, from 4-to-1 for infants to 12-to-1 for preschoolers, according to the operative Department of Defense Instruction.[2]

Yet, the current DoD fee structure does not recognize these cost differentials. Rather, it bases fees on total family income in an effort to make care affordable and realizing that infants grow into preschoolers who then average out their cost during their five-year stay in military child care. Because it is the youngest, lowest-earning families who tend to have the youngest children, fee income from the parents of infants is likely to be even less per child than fee income from the parents of older children. As a result, the DoD bears a larger cost burden for the CDC care of younger children. Yet, infants and pre-toddlers may be precisely the children that CDCs *should* serve in a community because their care is the most costly. In addition, the number of slots that is available for infant care in any given community is usually far less than the number of slots that is available for older children. If the government wants to promote more care for infants, it must accept the higher cost per child associated with infant

---

[2]DoDI 6060.2, para. E.4.2.1.

care. Another option, discussed later in this chapter, is to strongly promote infant and pre-toddler care in FCC.

CHILD DEVELOPMENT CENTER CARE

Our work demonstrates once again that care in centers is particularly costly. Our analyses reveal that costs across centers vary substantially, and we highlighted some differences across Military Services. We did not observe a consistent difference between the cost of contractor-operated versus DoD-operated centers. This suggests that using a contractor will not necessarily save the DoD money.

This conclusion that money will not necessarily be saved by outsourcing is important input to the outsourcing debate. According to OMB Circular A-76, the federal government can outsource an activity to a contractor following a competitive bidding process only if the contracted costs are at least 10 percent lower than the government's proposed cost.[3]

In the competition process, both the government and contractor proposals must meet the same quality specifications. Our results and the results of an A-76 MEO competition in San Diego (discussed later in this section) suggest that A-76 studies of DoD child care will not lead to much outsourcing because accredited care cannot be provided at a significantly lower cost than what the government currently spends.

At the same time, Gates and Robbert (2000) find that A-76 studies, while costly to implement, do generate cost savings, even if the activity remains in-house. In the process of developing the MEO, government organizations typically identify opportunities for cost savings, primarily by finding ways to do the same work with fewer people. In the child-care area, such labor cost savings are inherently limited by child-to-staff ratio requirements, which apply to contractors and the DoD alike. The staffing ratios place a limit on the cost

---

[3]The "10-percent rule" is designed to ensure that the government does not initiate an outsourcing effort, which is often associated with significant transition costs and staff turnover, in pursuit of small savings. See Robbert, Gates, and Elliott (1997) for more information.

savings that can be generated through competitive pressure in the child-care area.

Cost differences across centers appear to be significantly influenced by the number of children being served in a given center, with lower per-child costs in larger centers. CDC costs are also influenced by the cost of living in the local area, with higher per-child costs observed at installations located in areas with a high cost of living.

Our survey revealed dramatic differences across installations in the cost of care per child. For infants, we observed a few low-cost installations that were providing care for less than $7,000 per child, whereas the highest-cost installations were spending upwards of $20,000 per child. While some of the variation reflects idiosyncratic differences in expenditures (for example, one center went through a major renovation and all the excess costs were incurred in the study year), much of the variation is not explainable by such factors. This variation represents a useful opportunity for DoD CDCs to learn from one another and potentially identify opportunities to reduce costs without sacrificing quality.

The DoD runs one of the largest and most highly regarded systems of child care in the country, and is continuing to improve the system by highlighting and learning from cost and quality improvement efforts conducted in individual centers and regions and disseminating information on those efforts across the system. For example, the Navy's San Diego Region A-76 competition for an MEO suggested some potentially useful strategies for cost savings by streamlining administration for the entire region and reducing overstaffing. One important caveat in determining CDC costs stems from the difficulty we encountered in calculating CDC costs that fell into the "other" category. This difficulty reflects a larger problem in calculating both activity costs in the DoD and child-care costs in any setting; it is in no way a problem unique to DoD CDCs. Respondents to our cost survey often did not have all the administrative information that we requested. Our estimates of "other costs" are correspondingly less than fully accurate.

This dearth of administrative information reflects a larger problem: No systems are in place to monitor the cost of existing programs; therefore, program managers often do not have complete cost information. This lack of essential information makes it very difficult to come to management decisions that would improve efficiency without sacrificing quality. One reason that this information is not available is that, in the past, financial information was collected and disseminated primarily to ensure that activities managers did not overspend their appropriation. The idea of using cost information to improve the effectiveness and efficiency of the organization was secondary to not overspending the budget (Gates and Robbert, 2000).

To some degree, this focus on providing information pertaining to present cost overruns still dominates the cost arena. In fact, Gates and Robbert (2000) found that none of the managers of programs that won a competitive sourcing competition (MEO winners) could provide complete cost information on the implemented MEO. When asked by the researchers to provide cost data, the program managers could only provide personnel authorization information. As Gates and Robbert note, such information provides an insufficient basis for monitoring and managing costs, even if there were incentives in the system to be efficient (and the authors also note that such incentives were strikingly absent). The DoD has recognized the importance of cost information to activities managers and has been making improvements in this area over the past several years.

FAMILY CHILD CARE

Our data indicate that the cost of care in FCC homes is considerably lower than the cost for CDC care. Cost is not so closely tied to child age in FCCs; consequently, cost savings for the youngest children are the most substantial. However, cost comparisons with CDCs must be made with caution because of some limitations in our data collection and subsequent analyses. In the case of CDCs, we are basing cost estimates on a fairly comprehensive description of costs, including salaries, fringes, overhead, and maintenance. In contrast, in the case of FCC costs, we are estimating costs based only on the sum of the parent fees and DoD expenditures needed to administer the program. As a result, the cost estimates that we reached for FCC must be understood to be somewhat different from those derived for CDCs. Our FCC cost estimates essentially answer the following question: How much are parents (and the government) paying to have their children cared for? (In using the word "their," we are referring to the parents of the 80 percent of children in FCC whose do pay for their children's care.)

The FCC cost estimate is not arrived at in quite the same way as the estimate for CDC care. With center-based care, we have a great deal more insight into how costs are allocated. Take food as an example. For CDC care, we are able to capture the full cost of delivering meals to children. This may include the cost of service personnel and supplies, in addition to the cost of the food itself. For our FCC estimate, we had to rely on the amount of monies being recouped from the USDA food program. All other costs associated with food preparation are essentially absorbed by the provider. For example, the energy needed to heat the oven and run other appliances, water to wash dishes, and wear and tear on kitchen utensils are not captured. The time to prepare a meal probably comes out of the time available for direct care, or may be donated by the provider if he or she prepares food in advance.

In addition, we don't know how much money providers are earning on a per-hour basis. In order to have obtained an estimate more analogous to that for CDC costs, we would have had to impute a wage rate to FCC providers. Such an imputation is difficult because many providers care for their own children along with those of others. Obviously, no one is paying a fee for those children. Yet, they are a part of the program (and we did include them in dividing up other costs).

CONTRACTOR-OPERATED CARE

In the DoD, contractor-operated care is provided through several types of arrangements, ranging from a plan that pays the difference between the DoD fee schedule and the fee at several accredited child-care centers in the local area, to a system in which the government subsidizes both the facilities and the parent fees.

The cost of contractor-operated care clearly falls within the range of costs observed for DoD-run care. The estimated cost per infant in the contractor-based centers is generally lower than the average cost per infant in DoD-run centers, whereas the cost per preschooler in the contractor-based centers is generally higher than the average cost per preschooler in DoD-run centers. There is, therefore, no evidence that contractor-run centers are either cheaper or more expensive than DoD-run centers.[4]

CIVILIAN EMPLOYER CARE

Our visits to civilian employer-sponsored centers helped to identify factors that lead to higher costs. In centers in which the employer doesn't question subsidy levels, care is provided under extremely low child-to-staff ratios, pay caregivers at higher rates, hire well-educated directors, and have stunningly attractive centers.

Those visits provided insights into the different approaches to running centers. For example, even the highest-quality contractors have moved to a system of regional curriculum advisors. They believe that through regionalization of this function, important local input into curriculum design can be maintained while the costs for better-educated, and therefore more costly, curriculum developers can be contained. These contractors devote less attention and resources to on-site training than DoD CDCs do.

These civilian centers also put the issue of cost differentials by child age into a broader perspective. All of these centers charged fees that vary as a function of a child's age. Our civilian interviewees believed that such differentials not only made sense but were also an important educational tool. More than one interviewee said explicitly that parents need to understand that taking care of an infant simply costs more than taking care of an older child, and therefore, centers need to charge higher fees for infants.[5]

IMPLICATIONS AND ISSUES

The fact that it costs more to care for an infant than an older child in a CDC, and that it costs *much* more to care for an infant in a CDC

---

[4]We emphasize that we did not examine the quality of the contractor-run centers, although we do note that they are all accredited.

[5]The DoD, of course, has a very different view on parent fees. Its overriding concern is to ensure that care is affordable to all families. Moreover, the DoD has built a longer time line into its fee structure. By linking fees to family income, fees *increase* over time, even as children age, which the DoD considers a fair way to assess fees without over-burdening families.

than in FCC, raises important questions and issues for the DoD. Key among them is this: What are the primary goals of military child care? If the primary goal is to serve as many children as possible given a fixed amount of funds, serving infants in CDCs makes little sense. Given a fee schedule that does not differentiate by child age, and given much higher costs for infant care than older-child care in CDCs, the current policy, which permits care for infants in CDCs, means that a great deal of money is being devoted to a small number of infants.[6] If these same infants were cared for in FCC, the program could serve substantially more children for the same cost. If, on the other hand, the primary goal is to allow parents to choose among care settings and select the type of care they prefer (and, if families have multiple children, allow the children to be cared for in the same location), then having infant slots in CDCs (as well as FCC) makes sense.

Even if the DoD decided to more aggressively promote FCC infant care, it is not clear that it would be easy to increase the supply of FCC slots, even with increased subsidies. Most military spouses are already employed, are in school, or are not looking for work. Many potential providers have college degrees and are looking for work on a career track; others want only part-time work that does not interfere with their own family life.

The Services are actively pursuing new FCC models that address the concerns of both would-be providers and parents. For example, the Army has created some group homes, which provide home-based care for twice or even three times as many children as the standard FCC home. Such homes make providers less isolated and give parents more stability and greater oversight. The Air Force and the Army are offering "wraparound care" in nearby homes for children in CDCs whose parents need extended hours care. Providers transport children to and from the CDC, which reduces the parental burden (see Zellman et al., 1992). An important element of the San Diego MEO was a 50-percent reduction in the number of infants and toddlers cared for in CDCs and a concurrent increase in FCC slots for

---

[6]Some installations, in recognizing this situation, have chosen not to serve infants in CDCs and refer them to FCC instead.

those children. FCC slots were to be increased through an aggressive recruitment and subsidization program.

All of these new approaches must be implemented in a way that reflects specific local needs and relies on local resources. An approach that works in a large metropolitan area with a large number of military personnel, such as San Diego, might be useless in a remote installation, such as Minot Air Force Base in northern North Dakota.

Another important DoD child-care goal, as reflected in its fee policy, is to provide *affordable* child care to military families. The DoD certainly achieves this goal, if its fees are compared against the fees that we encountered in the private employer-sponsored centers. Our cost analyses make clear that the DoD achieves this goal through a substantial subsidy, which varies with child age, and that subsidy is most generous for the parents of infants.[7]

To its credit, the DoD has achieved affordability without sacrificing quality. The high rate of accreditation of DoD centers attests to the quality built into the system (Zellman and Johansen, 1996).

And the DoD has done all of this while providing care to many thousands of children. In this respect, the DoD's goals are far grander than those of any of the private-sector employers that we examined. For many of those employers, a showplace center and equitable access met their goals; the fact that the center served a small number of employees was not an issue.

Our research suggests that employers such as the DoD face complicated trade-offs in deciding whether and how to provide child care for the children of employees. Those employers must balance concerns of cost, quality, and access. Our data make it clear that the cost of providing center-based care is substantial, whether that care is provided by the DoD or by a contractor. However, the cost for this provision is not out of line with the costs associated with other employer-based centers.

Our results also suggest that outsourcing is unlikely to generate substantial cost savings in the child-care arena. Given the substantial

---

[7]Since costs are highest for infants but fees do not take into account child age, subsidies are highest for the youngest children.

costs associated with staging an A-76 competition and the small likelihood given the strict regulations (particularly the unyielding ratio requirements) that any contractor could provide care for 90 percent or less of what it costs the DoD, it seems unlikely that outsourcing will be a viable policy option. Other, more-complicated options must be considered.

We urge the DoD to use the cost data provided here in concert with clearly articulated child-care system goals to develop policy that will produce an optimal mix of child-care options. It is clear, for example, that FCC care, particularly for infants, is cost-effective. A more aggressive subsidy policy, and other approaches that the Services are currently pursuing, could increase the attractiveness of this option to both parents and providers. Our data also indicate that CDC size is an important cost driver. The DoD may want to develop policy that encourages larger and more cost-efficient CDCs.

The military child-care system provides high-quality care to large numbers of children. Generous subsidies enable this care to be affordable as well. With the cost data provided in this report, the DoD has an additional tool at its disposal that can help it further improve system efficiency, affordability, and reach—all of which have made military child care a model for the nation.

CHILD-CARE COST SURVEY

The following pages contain a copy of the Child-Care Cost Survey administered to the Navy. The surveys for the other Services (Air Force, Army, Contractor, and Marine Corps) vary slightly in wording to reflect differences in service terminology.

RCS DD-P&R(OT)2078 exp. 4/28/00 - NAV

SURVEY OF CHILD DEVELOPMENT PROGRAM COSTS

I. Introduction

This survey requests cost and enrollment information on Child Development Center (CDC), Family Child Care (FCC) and School Age Care (SAC) activities of the child development program. We would like you to provide information for all of FY `98 (October `97 through September `98). Provide information on SAC only if the SAC program is run by the child development program. If SAC is run by the Youth Program, please do not report on SAC anywhere in this survey. Please complete each question as indicated.

1. Installation Name: _____   1 – 3 /

2. Number of separate, free-standing CDCs in FY `98: _____   6 /

3. Did the child development program provide School Age Care (SAC) in FY `98
    In CDCs
      Yes..........................☐   7 /
      No...........................☐

    In other locations (e.g. Youth Centers, Schools)
      Yes..........................☐   8 /
      No...........................☐

II. Personnel Costs

In this section we ask you to provide specific information about personnel costs related to CDC and FCC activity.

We ask you to provide cost information for each center separately. If this is not possible, provide the total for all centers in the column provided.

Before you begin, please note that it is important to distinguish between center level and program level personnel as you complete this form. We describe the distinction below.

Center level personnel are government employees who work in CDCs and have no work responsibilities other than those directly related to the activity of one or more centers.

Center level personnel include direct care givers, center directors and assistant directors, and training and curriculum specialists. Center level personnel might also include food service workers and custodians, if these people are employed by your program. Do not include contract workers or general base operating support employees in Table 1 on center level personnel.

1

Most center level personnel will work in one and only one center. However, some may spread their time across several centers. For individuals who work in several centers, please allocate the costs of that individual to centers in proportion to your best estimate of the time they spend working at that center. For example, if a custodian works six hours per day at Center #1 and two hours per day at Center #2, you would allocate 3/4 of the cost of that individual to Center #1 and 1/4 of the cost to Center #2.

Program level personnel are government employees who work in the Child Development area and perform functions that contribute to the activities of CDCs, SAC, and/or FCC. Some might also spend at least some of their time working in, managing, or servicing functions other than child development programs (e.g., Youth Programs), but this is not necessary to be considered a program-level staffer. These individuals should not appear on the center level personnel budget (Table 1).

Program level personnel include the director of the Child Development program, and other administrative and support staff in the Child Development office. Such personnel might also include training and curriculum specialists who work with FCC as well as in CDCs. In the case of a contracted service, it might also include a contracting officer and/or the contracting officer's representative. Program level personnel should be included in Table 2.

CARD 01

2

Center Level Personnel Costs

2.1   Please enter total personnel costs for each category of personnel listed in Table 1 by center for FY `98, which includes the period from October 1 1997 to September 30, 1998. Total personnel costs include wages, benefits, and any training costs.

Fill in the last column only if your child development program provides classroom-based SAC outside of CDCs. If SAC is provided in the CDC, include those costs in the main part of Table 1. If SAC is provided by the youth program, do not report SAC information on Table 1.

We realize that some CDC budgets do not break out personnel costs in the way we need. Please look now at Table 1. If your budget information allows you to complete this table, please do so now and ignore Optional Worksheet for Table 1. If not, you may use Optional Worksheet for Table 1 to help you perform these calculations.

Table 1
Total Center Level Personnel Costs by Center
FY `98

	Center #1	Center #2	Center #3	Center #4	All Centers (complete only if data by center is not available)	Classroom based SAC run by CDS and provided outside CDCs	
APF Direct Care Staff							
NAF Direct Care Staff							
Food Preparation/ Service Employees							CARD 02 4-5 / 1-3 /
Center Directors, Assistant Directors, Clerks, Custodians							
Training & Curriculum Specialists							CARD 03 4-5 / 1-3 /
Other Center level Personnel (specify type)							

3

Program Level Personnel Costs

(CARD 04)   4-5 /
              1-3 /

2.2   Please list the position title of all child development program level employees,
      provide personnel cost information for each employee and provide your <u>best</u>
      <u>estimate</u> of the fraction of time these individuals spend in different activities
      including contract-related activities (e.g., monitoring the contractor, responding to
      complaints), if applicable. Please note that these fractions need not account for all
      (100%) of an individual's time. Please report whether the cost of this individual is
      reflected in the child development program budget. <u>None</u> of the individuals
      included in this table should have been included in Table 1.

Please report annual data for FY `98.

Table 2
Total Program Level Personnel Costs
FY `98

Position Title	Grade level (provide GS level if appropriate)	Total personnel cost	Fraction of work time devoted to CDC activities	Fraction of work time devoted to FCC activities	Fraction of work time devoted to SAC activities	Fraction of work time devoted to contract-related activities (if applicable)	Cost of this position appears in which budget? 1: CDC 2: FCC 3: SAS 4: CDP Admin 5: Other (enter number)
#1							
#2							
#3							
#4							
#5							
#6							
#7							
#8							

CARD 05
4-5 /
1-3 /

CARD 06
4-5 /
1-3 /

4

III. Number of Children Served on a Weekly Fee Basis in CDCs and SAC

In this section we ask you about the number of children enrolled on a weekly fee basis by each CDC and SAC program on your installation and the capacity of these programs. We request information for contractor operated CDCs as well as government operated centers. This section pertains only to children enrolled on a weekly fee basis. Children enrolled on an hourly fee basis will be recorded in section IV. We ask you to report information on full-time and part-time attendees separately. Table 3 includes only children enrolled on a full-time weekly fee basis. Table 5 includes only children enrolled on a part-time weekly fee basis. We also ask you to provide enrollment information for each center separately. If this is not possible, provide the total for all centers in the column provided.

3.1   Report the number of children enrolled full-time on a weekly fee basis during one of the two two-week pay periods between March 1 and March 28, 1998 for each center by age group in Table 3. Include only children who are enrolled on a regular and continuing basis. Do not include slots reserved for hourly care. Do not include SAC in Table 3; it will be covered in Table 5. We understand that enrollment may vary at certain times of the year, and ask you to describe that variation in a later item (3.3).

(CARD 07)   4-5 /
1-3 /

Table 3
Total Number of Children Enrolled Full-Time on a Weekly Fee Basis in CDCs
March, 1998

	Center #1	Center #2	Center #3	Center #4	All Centers (complete only if data by center is not available)	Numbers consistent over the course of the year? (yes or no)
Infant						
Pre-toddler						
Toddler						
Pre-school						

3.2   In Table 4 report each center's operational capacity for serving children in each age group during one of the two-week pay periods between March 1 and March 28, 1998. Report the operational capacity only for rooms that were actually in use for the provision of child care at that time.

5

Table 4
Operational Capacity by Center and Age Group
March, 1998

	Center #1	Center #2	Center #3	Center #4
Infant				
Pre-toddler				
Toddler				
Pre-school				

CARD 08   4-5 /
1-3 /

3.3 If the number of children enrolled is not consistent over the course of the year, please describe the variation both in terms of when it occurs, its magnitude (e.g., "in August we have half as many children as we do in other months because of PCS moves"), and the age groups most impacted.

6 /

_____

_____

_____

_____

_____

_____

3.4 If the number of children enrolled (Table 3) differs from capacity (Table 4) please explain.

7 /

_____

_____

_____

_____

_____

_____

6

3.5   In Table 5, please describe the <u>part-time</u> programs including enrichment programs operated by the child development program that enroll children on a weekly fee basis. For each program, please report the number of children enrolled during one of the two two-week pay periods between March 1 and March 28, 1998, the number of hours of care per child per week, the age group (infant, pre-toddler, toddler, pre-school, school-age) of the children served, and the center that operates the program (use the same numbers as in Table 1). If the child development program operates a SAC program in a location other than a center, note that location in the last column. If a program serves children in more than one age group, please report the number served in each age group separately on the lines provided.

Table 5
Part-Time CDC Programs Serving Children on a Weekly Fee Basis
March, 1998

Program Description (include hours per day, days per week)	# of Children Enrolled (per session)	Age Group	Costs of running this program are in which budget? (Center #, SAC program, other)

CARD 09   4-5 /
           1-3 /

7

IV. Children Served on an Hourly Fee Basis in CDCs

In this section we ask about care provided on an <u>hourly fee basis</u> during one of the two two-week pay periods from March 1 to March 28, 1998. We are interested in dedicated hourly care "slots" rather than the actual number of children served. An hourly care "slot" is a space available all day for hourly care. Several children may be served by one slot on a given day (e.g., 0800-1000; 1100-1400; 1400-1600). If a space is available for hourly care only 1/2 day, count it as 1/2 a slot. If your CDCs provide no hourly care, or only provide hourly care when space in a full-time slot is not being used, check the box either in item 4.1 or 4.2, and leave Table 6 blank.

4.1　No hourly care slots available in CDCs on this
installation.　　　　　　　　　　☐ → skip to Section V, page 9.　　　44 /

4.2　Hourly care is available in CDCs on this installation <u>only</u>
when full-time slots are open.　　☐ → skip to Section V, page 9.　　45 /

4.3　If you did not check either of the above two boxes, please record the number of dedicated hourly care slots by age group in Table 6 below. <u>Do not</u> include hourly care provided on a "space available" basis in regular classrooms (e.g., when a full-time child is sick).

Table 6
Total Number of Dedicated Hourly Care Slots in CDCs
March, 1998

	Center #1	Center #2	Center #3	Center #4	All Centers (complete only if data by center is not available)	Number of slots consistent over the course of the year? (yes/no)
Infant						
Pre-toddler						
Toddler						
Pre-school						
School-age						

CARD 10　　4-5
　　　　　　1-3

8

V. Family Child Care

In this section we ask you some questions about family child care. We ask you to provide information for one of the two two-week pay periods between March 1 and March 28, 1998.

5.1 Select one of the two two-week pay periods between March 1 and March 28 and report the # of licensed FCC homes as of that period.

☐ ☐ ☐   30-32 /

5.2. Distinguishing between the FCC providers' own children and the children of others, report the number of children enrolled in FCC by child age group in Table 7.

Table 7
Family Child Care Provided
March, 1998

Child Age	# of Providers' own children served	# of other children served	Average # of hours of care per child per day
Infant			
Pre Toddler			
Toddler			
Pre-School			
School Age			

5.3 Please report the average (per child) weekly parent fee paid to licensed FCC providers in FY `98 by child age in Table 8 below.

(CARD 11)   4-5 /
                1-3 /

Table 8
Family Child Care Fee Information
FY `98

Child Age	Average Weekly Parent Fee for Full-time Care	
Infant		6-8 /
Pre-Toddler		9-11 /
Toddler		12-14 /
Pre-School		15-17 /
School Age		18-20 /
Other (specify)		21-23 /

9

5.4 Does your installation provide cash subsidies other than USDA Reimbursement to FCC providers?

No.............................☐ → skip to Section VI, page 11.　24 /

Yes....⸲.....................☐

5.5 Please report the average weekly per child cash subsidy given to FCC providers in FY '98.

Table 9
Average Cash Subsidy to FCC Providers
FY `98

Child Age	Average Cash Subsidy	
Infant		25-26 /
Pre-Toddler		27-28 /
Toddler		29-30 /
Pre-School		31-32 /
School Age		33-34 /
Other (specify)		35-37 /

VI. Budget Data

In this section we ask you to provide government (APF and NAF) expenditure data for all CDCs, SAC and FCC on your installation for FY `98. If you have a separate budget for program administration, please include that.

If you have an already-prepared expenditure report, you may submit that in lieu of filling out Tables 10 and 11. If you do not have a prepared report, please complete the table below. If you cannot provide information for all of FY `98 please provide information for one quarter in FY `98 and note that quarter at the top of the table. We are not requesting separate information for each center. Please report information on the USDA program payments to providers and CDCs in Table 12.

Table 10
FY `98 APF Expenditures

	CDC FY `98	FCC FY `98	SAC FY `98	Program Administration FY `98	
Military Personnel					
Civilian Personnel					
Travel of Personnel					CARD 12
Transportation of Things					4-5 / 1-3 /
Utilities					
Communications					
Rent					CARD 13
Maintenance and Repair					4-5 / 1-3 /
Service Contracts					
Supplies					CARD 14
Equipment					4-5 / 1-3 /
Minor Construction					
USA Expenses					CARD 15
Other Expenses					4-5 / 1-3 /
Total					

CARD 16   4-5 /
           1-3 /

Table 11
FY `98 NAF Expenditures

	CDC FY `98	FCC FY `98	SAC FY `98	Program Administration FY `98
NAF Personnel				
NAF Payroll				
401 K				
FICA Tax				
Group Insurance				
U.S. Citizens' Benefits				
Worker's Compensation				
Payroll – Sick Leave Taken				
Unemployment Compensation				
Annual Leave				
Retirement Benefits				
Other				
Total NAF Personnel				
Non-Personnel				
Supply Expenses (including food)				
Maintenance and Repair				
Postage, Subscriptions, Dues				
Coupons and Advertising				
Bank Fees and Charges				
Credit Card Expenses				
Misc. Operating Expenses				
Printing, Reproduction				
Depreciation/Amortization				
Other Non-Personnel Expenses				
Total Non-Personnel				
TOTAL				

CARD 17
4-5 /
1-3 /

CARD 18
4-5 /
1-3 /

CARD 19
4-5 /
1-3 /

CARD 20
4-5 /
1-3 /

CARD 21
4-5 /
1-3 /

Table 12
USDA Program Expenditures FY `98

Payments to CDCs	Payments to FCC Providers	Payments to SAC (if stand-alone)

CARD 22   4-5 /
1-3 /

VII. Additional Questions

7.1   Did any of the CDCs on this installation provide care outside of your centers'
standard operating hours during FY `98—weekend or extended hours?

No..............................☐-→ Go to question 7.4   6 /
Yes......................…........☐

7.2   If Yes, are the costs of personnel performing that care reflected in the costs reported
above ?

No..............................☐-→ Go to question 7.4   7 /
Yes......................…........☐

7.3   If Yes, how many hours of such care were provided? Can you provide an estimate
of the cost of providing this care?

Number of hours of supplemental

care FY `98 ....☐☐☐☐☐ hours   8-12 /

Estimated cost of providing supplemental care

in FY `98........................ $ ☐,☐☐☐,☐☐☐   13-19 /

Where does the cost of providing this care appear?
(e.g. CDC #1 Budget) _____   20 /

7.4   Did you have any contracts with an external provider for center-based child care at
any time during FY `98?

No..............................☐-→ Go to question 7.6
Yes......................…........☐   21 /

7.5   If Yes, what was the annual cost of those contracts for FY `98? Please indicate the
cost and the period covered.

Total contract cost ... $ ☐☐,☐☐☐,☐☐☐   22-29 /

Period covered .... from ☐☐ / ☐☐ / ☐☐   30-35 /

to ☐☐ / ☐☐ / ☐☐   36-41 /

13

7.6 Were custodial services provided to CDC contractors on this installation through a contract arrangement or a base-wide custodial pool?

  No....☐-→ go to question 7.8   42 /
  Yes...☐

7.7 If Yes, were the costs reflected in Table 10 or 11 on APF and NAF Expenditures?

  No..............................☐   43 /
  Yes.............................☐

7.8 Please describe any special circumstances on your installation (e.g., deployment) that necessitated the provision of child care in FY `98 beyond the normal level.

_____   44 /
_____
_____
_____
_____

7.9 Please provide your name, title, and commercial phone number in case we need to call for clarification.

Name:_____

Title:_____

Phone #:_____

THANK YOU SO MUCH FOR COMPLETING THIS QUESTIONNAIRE!

Please return it to RAND in the self-addressed postage paid envelope.

CARD 22

REGRESSION ANALYSIS OF COST PER CHILD BY AGE GROUP

As we have discussed in this report, the existing literature and common sense suggested some initial hypotheses that relate the cost of CDC care to certain aspects of the setting in which that care is provided. Specifically, we hypothesized that larger centers might have a lower cost per child due to their economies of scale, centers located in areas with a high cost of living would have greater care costs because of their higher wage rates for caregivers, and centers in remote areas might have greater care costs because they might have to pay higher wages to attract caregivers to their remote locations.

It was also hypothesized that costs would vary by Military Service, based on Service reports on APF funding of child-care slots. To analyze the relationship between these factors and cost, we conducted a simple regression analysis. We modeled the cost per child as a linear function, as follows:

$$\text{Cost per child} = \alpha + \beta_1 \text{Army} + \beta_2 \text{AirForce} + \beta_3 \text{Navy} + \beta_4 \ln(\text{medinc}) + \beta_5 \text{Remote} + \beta_6 \text{Size} + \beta_7 \text{Percentyoung} + \varepsilon$$

Army, Air Force, Navy,[1] and *Remote* are dummy variables that take on a value of 1 if the CDC is located on an installation that has that characteristic and take on a value of 0 otherwise. *Ln(medinc)* is a continuous variable reflecting the natural logarithm of the median income in the local area (the SMSA) in which the installation is located. *Size* is a continuous variable reflecting the average enrollment

---

[1] The Marine Corps is omitted from each equation.

of the child-care centers on the installation (number of full-time equivalent [FTE] children enrolled, divided by the number of centers). *Percentyoung* is a continuous variable reflecting the percentage of total center enrollment accounted for by infants and pre-toddlers. We estimated several cost equations, using different dependent variables. First, we analyzed the total annual cost for each age group.[2] We then conducted a regression analysis on the separate components of cost discussed in Chapter Four: other cost per child, food cost per child, and direct labor cost per child. Regression results are reported later in this appendix. In reporting the results on direct labor cost per child, we give only the results for infants and simply note that the results for infants mirror those for other age groups.

ANNUAL COST PER CHILD BY AGE GROUP

For each age group, the parameter estimates on average center size are negative and significant at the 1-percent level (see Tables B.1 through B.4). Installations with more children per center have lower per-child operating costs. The parameter estimate on average size is –21 for infants, indicating that if Installation A, for instance, has ten more children per center than Installation B, all other things being equal, Installation A's annual cost per infant will be $210 per year lower. This negative relationship between center size and cost applied to all age groups. We tested for nonlinear relationships between average center size and cost, but the linear model provided a better fit, suggesting that within the range of the observed data (centers with 54 to 341 children and a median size of 150 children), there are economies of scale to be exploited.

The cost of living in the local area also appears to impact costs. For each age group, the parameter estimate on *ln(income)* was positive and significant at the 10-percent (but not at the 5-percent) level. This suggests that installations located in areas with a higher cost of living have higher annual operating costs.

---

[2]We do not conduct a regression analysis for school-age care because only ten of the installations offered school-age care in the CDCs and, therefore, the parameter estimates were not significant.

Table B.1

Analysis of Cost per Infant

	Degrees of Freedom	Sum of Squares
Regression	7	330943141
Residual	50	544167905
Total	57	875111046

	Coefficient	Standard Error	T-statistic	P-value
Intercept	−25526.18	18737.22	−1.362	0.179
Army	1431.811	1540.386	0.930	0.357
Air Force	2955.154	1537.023	1.923	0.060
Navy	2957.932	1600.012	1.849	0.070
Median income	3520.12	1763.894	1.996	0.051
Remoteness	−117.813	1038.69	−0.113	0.910
Average center size	−22.50853	6.784662	−3.318	0.002
Percentage of infants and pre-toddlers	10254.42	7783.455	1.317	0.194

NOTE: Number of observations = 58. R-squared = 0.3782.

Table B.2

Analysis of Cost per Pre-toddler

	Degrees of Freedom	Sum of Squares
Regression	7	258393983
Residual	50	489130292
Total	57	747524275

	Coefficient	Standard Error	T-statistic	P-value
Intercept	−23504.57	17458.98	−1.346	0.184
Army	1437.754	1435.302	1.002	0.321
Air Force	2647.505	1432.168	1.849	0.070
Navy	2628.949	1490.86	1.763	0.084
Median income	3212.979	1643.562	1.955	0.056
Remoteness	−230.2143	967.8315	−0.238	0.813
Average center size	−21.01294	6.321817	−3.324	0.002
Percentage of infants and pre-toddlers	9634.509	7252.473	1.328	0.190

NOTE: Number of observations = 58. R-squared = 0.3680.

Table B.3

Analysis of Cost per Toddler

	Degrees of Freedom	Sum of Squares
Regression	7	211309392
Residual	51	370338021
Total	58	581647413

	Coefficient	Standard Error	T-statistic	P-value
Intercept	−20179.73	15201.63	−1.327	0.190
Army	1215.98	1256.537	0.968	0.338
Air Force	2192.872	1252.314	1.751	0.086
Navy	2264.796	1299.164	1.743	0.087
Median income	2726.593	1437.187	1.897	0.063
Remoteness	−327.2508	830.1784	−0.394	0.695
Average center size	−18.40343	5.53198	−3.327	0.002
Percentage of infants and pre-toddlers	7989.061	5636.365	1.417	0.162

NOTE: Number of observations = 59. R-squared = 0.3633.

Table B.4

Analysis of Cost per Preschooler

	Degrees of Freedom	Sum of Squares
Regression	7	153382410
Residual	51	285643359
Total	58	439025769

	Coefficient	Standard Error	T-statistic	P-value
Intercept	−16914.47	13350.67	−1.267	0.211
Army	977.6788	1103.54	0.886	0.380
Air Force	1709.35	1099.832	1.554	0.126
Navy	1869.599	1140.977	1.639	0.107
Median income	2231.315	1262.194	1.768	0.083
Remoteness	−408.8148	729.0953	−0.561	0.577
Average center size	−15.72219	4.858403	−3.236	0.002
Percentage of infants and pre-toddlers	6602.974	4950.078	1.334	0.188

NOTE: Number of observations = 59. R-squared = 0.3494.

Our regressions also suggest some differences across Services. For infants, pre-toddlers and toddlers, the parameter estimates on *Navy* and *Air Force* are positive and significant at the 10-percent (but not at the 5-percent) level, suggesting that the cost per child is higher in the Navy and Air Force than it is in the Marine Corps for all age groups. Holding other factors constant, the annual cost of infant care at a Marine Corps installation is nearly $3,000 less than at a Navy or Air Force installation.

Remoteness of an installation and the percentage of infants and pre-toddlers did not have a measurable effect on cost.

ANALYSIS OF COST COMPONENTS

We also estimated separate regression equations for the three cost components: other costs per child, food costs per child, and direct labor costs per child. As discussed in Chapter Three, we calculated a single value for other cost per child and food cost per child for each installation; these estimates do not vary by child age. Direct labor cost estimates were calculated separately by child age, as described in Chapter Three. In reporting the regression results on direct labor cost per child, we give only the results for infants and simply note that the results for infants mirror those for other age groups.

The regression results on the individual cost components are presented in Tables B.5 through B.7. They provide some additional insight into the factors driving the results presented earlier in this appendix. First, we observe that installations with more children per center have lower other costs and lower direct-care labor costs. This suggests that larger centers, through economies of scale and through a more efficient use of staff, are able to reduce the cost per child for indirect and administrative costs. These relationships are significant at the 1-percent level. For other costs, the parameter estimate on average size is –11, indicating that if Installation A, for instance, has ten more children per center than Installation B, then all other things being equal, Installation A's annual other cost per infant will be $110 per year lower. We also observe a small negative relationship between average center size and food cost per child that is significant at the 10-percent level.

Table B.5

Analysis of Other Costs per Child

	Degrees of Freedom	Sum of Squares
Regression	7	85024061.3
Residual	51	186403245
Total	58	271427307

	Coefficient	Standard Error	T-statistic	P-value
Intercept	−11725.32	10784.94	−1.087	0.282
Army	434.1357	891.4617	0.487	0.628
Air Force	928.7167	888.4663	1.045	0.301
Navy	1305.055	921.7039	1.416	0.163
Median income	1434.974	1019.626	1.407	0.165
Remoteness	−468.9281	588.9779	−0.796	0.430
Average center size	−11.23112	3.924716	−2.862	0.006
Percentage of infants and pre-toddlers	4289.251	3998.772	1.073	0.288

NOTE: Number of observations = 59. R-squared = 0.3132.

Table B.6

Analysis of Food Cost per Child

	Degrees of Freedom	Sum of Squares
Regression	7	411390.35
Residual	51	2276726.72
Total	58	2688117.08

	Coefficient	Standard Error	T-statistic	P-value
Intercept	−617.7862	1191.918	−0.518	0.606
Army	209.9207	98.52159	2.131	0.038
Air Force	103.7022	98.19055	1.056	0.296
Navy	11.26796	101.8639	0.111	0.912
Median income	102.9533	112.6859	0.914	0.365
Remoteness	−54.07627	65.09201	−0.831	0.410
Average center size	−0.7373302	0.4337474	−1.700	0.095
Percentage of infants and pre-toddlers	373.2009	441.932	0.844	0.402

NOTE: Number of observations = 59. R-squared = 0.2618.

Table B.7

Analysis of Direct-Care Labor Cost per Infant

	Degrees of Freedom	Sum of Squares
Regression	7	87550251.0
Residual	51	195872829
Total	58	283423080

	Coefficient	Standard Error	T-statistic	P-value
Intercept	-13714.1	11055.49	-1.240	0.220
Army	1000.867	913.825	1.095	0.279
Air Force	2030.794	910.7545	2.230	0.030
Navy	1659.827	944.8259	1.757	0.085
Median income	2080.165	1045.204	1.990	0.052
Remoteness	342.5687	603.7531	0.567	0.573
Average center size	-11.2612	4.023172	-2.799	0.007
Percentage of infants and pre-toddlers	5821.565	4099.086	1.420	0.162

NOTE: Number of observations = 59. R-squared = 0.3089.

No other variables are significant in the estimation of other costs per child. In particular, there are no significant differences across Services. With respect to food cost per child, *Army* is positive and significant at the 5-percent level. The Army food costs are $210 per child higher than the food costs for the Marine Corps. This could reflect differences in how food costs are accounted for or the fact that the Army provides formula for infants.

The cost of living in the local area appears to impact only direct-care labor costs. The parameter estimate for direct-care infant labor costs on *ln(income)* was positive and significant at the 5-percent level. This is not surprising in view of the fact that federal government wages are tied to a locale's cost of living through locality pay.

Our regressions also suggest that the Service differences reported earlier in this appendix are primarily driven by differences in direct-care labor costs. For infants, the parameter estimates on *Air Force* are positive and significant at the 5-percent level, and the estimates on *Navy* are positive and significant at the 10-percent (but not the 5-percent) level, suggesting that the cost per child is higher in the Navy and Air Force than it is in the Marine Corps.

Belkin, L., "Your Kids Are Their Problem," *New York Times Magazine*, July 23, 2000.

Belsky, J., "Two Waves of Day Care Research: Developmental Effects and Conditions of Quality," in R. C. Anslie, ed., *The Child and the Day Care Setting*, New York: Praeger, 1984.

Benken, E., Air Force Chief Master Sergeant, testimony at the Hearing of the Military Construction Subcommittee of the House Appropriations Committee, March 5, 1998.

Blank, H., A. Behr, and K. Schulman, *State Developments in Child Care, Early Education, and School-Age Care*, Washington, D.C.: Children's Defense Fund, 2000.

Bredekamp, S., "The Reliability and Validity of the Early Childhood Classroom Observation Scale for Accrediting Early Childhood Programs," *Early Childhood Research Quarterly*, Vol. 1, 1986, pp. 103–118.

Bright Horizons, *Solutions*, Cambridge, Mass.: Bright Horizons, Winter 1999.

Burud & Associates, *National Trend Study of Work-Site Child Care: Work-Site Child Care Today*, El Segundo, Calif.: Burud & Associates, 1996.

Campbell, N. D., J. Appelbaum, K. Martinson, and E. Martin, *Be All That We Can Be: Lessons from the Military for Improving Our*

Nation's Child Care System, Washington, D.C.: National Women's Law Center, 2000.

Chipty, T., "Economic Effects of Quality Regulations in the Day-Care Industry," *AEA Papers and Proceedings*, Vol. 85, No. 2, 1995, pp. 419–424.

Cost, Quality, and Child Outcomes Study Team, *Cost Quality and Child Outcomes in Child Care Centers, Public Report*, University of Colorado, Denver, 1995.

Culkin, M., J. R. Morris, and S. W. Helburn, "Quality and the True Cost of Child Care," *Journal of Social Issues*, Vol. 47, No. 2, 1991, pp. 71–86.

DHHS. *See* U.S. Department of Health and Human Services.

DoD. *See* U.S. Department of Defense.

Friedman, D., and B. Umland, *Survey of Work/Life Initiatives, 1998*, New York: William H. Mercer Companies LLC, and Cambridge, Mass.: Bright Horizons Family Solutions, 1998.

GAO. *See* U.S. General Accounting Office.

Gates, S. M., and A. A. Robbert, *Personnel Savings in Competitively Sourced DoD Activities: Are They Real? Will They Last?* Santa Monica, Calif.: RAND, MR-1117-OSD, 2000.

Hill-Scott, K., *Which Way, L.A.?* interview on KCRW Radio, Santa Monica, Calif., June 20, 2000.

Macro International, Inc., *1999 Family Child Care Research Project Report and Recommendations*, prepared for the Bureau of Naval Personnel, Morale, Welfare and Recreation Division, Calverton, Md., July 1999.

Mocan, H. N., "Cost Functions, Efficiency, and Quality in Day Care Centers," *The Journal of Human Resources*, Vol. 32, No. 4, Fall 1997, pp. 861–891.

Mukerjee, S., and A. D. White, "Provision of Child Care: Cost Functions for Profit-Making and Not-for-Profit Day Care Centers," *The Journal of Productivity Analysis*, Vol. 4, 1993, pp. 145–163.

National Association for the Education of Young Children, *Accreditation Criteria and Procedures of the National Academy of Early Childhood Programs*, Washington, D.C.: NAEYC, 1998.

Pint, E. M., and L. H. Baldwin, *Strategic Sourcing: Theory and Evidence from Economics and Business Management*, Santa Monica, Calif.: RAND, MR-865-AF, 1997.

Price, D., Educare CEO, personal communications, 2000.

Robbert, A. A., S. M. Gates, and M. N. Elliott, *Outsourcing of DoD Commercial Activities: Impacts on Civil Service Employees*, Santa Monica, Calif.: RAND, MR-866-OSD, 1997.

Schulman, K., *The High Cost of Child Care Puts Quality Care Out of Reach for Many Families*, Washington, D.C.: Children's Defense Fund, 2000.

Smith, K., *Who's Minding the Kids? Child Care Arrangements: Household Economic Studies*, Washington, D.C.: U.S. Census Bureau, October 2000.

U.S. Department of Defense, *Summary of FY 1999–2000 Child Care*, file report, 2000.

U.S. Department of Health and Human Services, *Access to Child Care for Low-Income Families*, 1999.

U.S. General Accounting Office, *Child Care: How Do Military and Civilian Center Costs Compare?* Washington, D.C.: General Accounting Office, GAO/HEHS-007, 1999.

Whitebook, M., C. Howes, and D. Phillips, *Worthy Work, Unlivable Wages, The National Child Care Staffing Study, 1988–1997*, Washington, D.C.: Center for the Child Care Workforce, 1998.

Zellman, G. L., and A. S. Johansen, "Military Child Care: Toward an Integrated Delivery System," *Armed Forces & Society*, Vol. 21, No. 4, 1995, pp. 639–659.

_____, "Investment or Overkill: Should Military Child Care Centers Be Accredited?" *Armed Forces & Society*, Vol. 23, 1996, pp. 249–268.

_____, *Examining the Implementation and Outcomes of the Military Child Care Act of 1989*, Santa Monica, Calif.: RAND, MR-665-OSD, 1998.

Zellman, G. L., A. S. Johansen, L. Meredith, and M. Selvin, *Improving the Delivery of Military Child Care: An Analysis of Current Operations and New Approaches*, Santa Monica, Calif.: RAND, R-4145-FMP, 1992.

Zellman, G. L., A. S. Johansen, and J. Van Winkle, *Examining the Effects of Accreditation on Military Child Development Center Operations and Outcomes*, Santa Monica, Calif.: RAND, MR-524-OSD, 1994.